MAN AND NATURE

An Anthropological Essay
in Human Ecology

The latest investigations respecting the early condition of the human race are tending to the conclusion that mankind commenced their career at the bottom of the scale and worked their way up from savagery to civilization through the slow accumulations of experimental knowledge.

Lewis Henry Morgan
the first paragraph of *Ancient Society* (1877)

MAN AND NATURE

An Anthropological Essay in Human Ecology

RICHARD A. WATSON
Washington University

PATTY JO WATSON
Washington University

HARCOURT, BRACE & WORLD, INC.
New York | Chicago | San Francisco | Atlanta

ISBN: 0-15-554725-9

Library of Congress Catalog Card Number: 72-76618

Printed in the United States of America

Cover photo by James Theologos

PREFACE

Man and Nature presents hypothetical models of eight ways of life —of the nonhuman primate, the protohuman, and six stages of man—synthesized from factual information about the interaction of selected primates with the physical environment. The eight "ways of life" chapters, which form Part II, the core of the book, thus contain few statements of "fact" in a technical sense. The models are constructed on the basis of fundamental laws derived from regularities observable in man's natural interaction with the physical environment and show the logical structure of the various forms of this interaction. Two introductory chapters—on methodology and terms, respectively—comprise Part I. Chapters 11 and 12, which make up Part III, evaluate the sequence of the models as a possible representation of evolutionary and historical fact.

Although the models are based on fact, we do not present them as representations of any actual ways of life; we claim only that they are reasonable generalizations of distinct types. They are meant to be altered in the light of further scientific discoveries. Their heuristic value lies in their representation of structural relations among elements within each type and among the various types. An examination of these structural relations may suggest courses of empirical investigation and can be used in testing syntheses in the field.

Similarly, the sequence of stages is not meant to represent an actual evolutionary or historical sequence. It does, however, proceed logically from simple to complex forms of interaction. This development is characterized by an increasing control over the physical environment, and thus by greater efficiency at providing food, at each successive stage, which eventually results in growth of population. A cultural environment is increasingly substituted for the physical environment as man succeeds in utilizing more and more powerful sources of energy.

Typological excesses have made anthropologists extremely sensitive to the fact that variety and continuity can be concealed by the lines of rigid classification. The reader should be aware, as we are, that all schemes of categories have dangers and limitations. Nevertheless, scientific investigation outside the framework of a preliminary conceptual structure of categories is impossible, no matter how tentative one's attachment to it may be. Just as the naive attempt to work outside categorial schemes cannot be condoned, neither can the attempt to impose ideal categories to which one's empirical observations are dogmatically required to conform. We do not intend our models to be taken dogmatically; they are not meant to be unalterable ideal types.

At the same time, we must insist that categorization is the foundation of rational thought. Men must categorize in order to understand, even when they have a minimum of particular factual data from which to generalize. The firmest conviction motivating us in our presentation is that one must always consciously recognize his categorial presuppositions when making an orderly study of the world. This can best be done by making explicit the specific categorial framework of the investigation. In anthropology, we must at times talk in terms of very extensive categories, even though we know that such concepts as "man" and "evolution" are extremely broad. Therefore, a few of our synthetic statements, very broad or very narrow or necessarily based on a small amount of factual data, may appear outrageous; many are the result of considered choice among plausible alternatives and are subject to informed disagreement; some, although they remain part of the overall synthesis, are so well established that they are acceptable as statements of fact. By building with available factual material, we show here some of the strengths and weaknesses of the primary categorial framework of anthropology, that of evolutionary development.

Several people were kind enough to take time from their own work to read the manuscript critically. Charles Leslie first set us to work on the project and has made helpful suggestions throughout. Frank Hole, Maxine R. Kleindienst, Barbara Lawrence, and James L. Watson have provided us with many detailed criticisms. Charles A. Reed was especially sensitive to problems of typology and his cautions about syntheses on this scale have made his comments invaluable. We wish to thank also Robert J. Braidwood, Richard H. Popkin, and Herbert E. Wright, Jr., none of whom read the manuscript but all of whom had important influences on its development. We alone, however, are responsible for any failure in this attempt to present model-building in anthropology as a neutral, essential, and valuable method, and to provide hypothetical models based on presently available factual knowledge that are open neither to outright rejection nor to uncritical acceptance, but to intelligent, constructive discussion.

During the completion of the manuscript, Richard A. Watson was concurrently a Fellow of the American Council of Learned Societies and of the Center for Advanced Study in the Behavioral Sciences, Stanford, California. These institutions made possible an incomparable year of study for both of us. We are particularly grateful to the Director of the Center, O. Meredith Wilson (who read and criticized the manuscript), and to his staff for their generous and most able assistance.

R. A. W.
P. J. W.

CONTENTS

xi

I

INTRO-
DUCTION

1 | METHODOLOGY

Anthropology is that part of natural science in which men study and attempt to understand man and his culture in a most general way. Since man is a part of nature, he can be studied scientifically and natural laws can be derived concerning his behavior, just as is the case for any other natural object. There are no logical differences between anthropology and physics, as branches of science. There are, however, differences in the degrees of confirmation of results attained by the physical sciences and the social sciences, and it is important to an understanding of the purposes and utility of the analyses in this book to have clearly in mind just how anthropology and physics, for example, are alike and how they differ.

Science is a search for laws pertaining to the characteristics and behavior of all natural objects. But before we can find laws, we must know the characteristics of objects. All knowledge depends on categorization, that is, the classification of objects according to their similarities to and differences from other objects. We know what a man is by recognizing what general characteristics an object must have (and must not have) in order for it to belong to the class called man. If one knows in a general way what a man is, he has the concept *man.* Concepts that are descriptive of objects are abstractions taken from our experience of the things of the world; they are an expression of man's ability to represent and consider particular things not only with respect to their uniqueness but also with respect to the characteristics they share with all other individuals of the same type. However, conceptual knowledge of the characteristics that are definitive of various classes or types of objects does not constitute scientific knowledge. Scientific knowledge is knowledge of generalizations, but scientific generalizations must describe not only the common characteristics of objects but also the common behavior of objects. Scientific knowledge is knowledge of scientific laws—laws that describe, in a general way, the common patterns of behavior exhibited by objects of similar kinds.

A scientific law has the following general form:

A. In circumstances of type *c,* all objects of type *o* exhibit a behavior pattern of type *b.*

To postulate such a universal law,[1] one must first have knowledge of the general characteristics definitive of objects of type *o* and evidence that in all known cases when an object of type *o* was in circumstances of type *c,* it exhibited a behavior pattern of type *b.* When such laws are based on induction from experience, they can never be established with certainty. Nor can laws based on logical rather than empirical grounds be established with certainty. No scientific law is known with certainty because every scientific law is a generalized description of behavior patterns of objects in the world that may or may not always exhibit the common behavior described. All scientific laws, therefore, are hypothetical postulations of varying

---

[1] Even so-called statistical laws are universal in the most general sense, i.e., a law of the form "In circumstances *c,* *x%* of objects of type *o* exhibit a behavior pattern of type *b*" is meant to hold universally for all objects of type *o.*

degrees of probability. We call these scientific laws *lawlike generalizations*. Such laws are established in practice, and we base our confidence in them on our continuing experience that objects do behave as the laws say they will. If our empirical investigations show that objects of type *o* do not typically exhibit a behavior pattern of type *b* in circumstances of type *c*, then we rightfully lose confidence in the accuracy and utility of the law and alter or discard it.

Lawlike generalizations of form A are said to be *causal* laws if the circumstances *c* or some aspect of them are said to be the cause *c'*, and the behavior pattern *b* or some aspect of it is said to be the effect *b'*.

Causal laws are of the following form:

B. In all cases where objects of type *o* are in circumstances of type *c*, circumstances of type *c'* cause a behavior pattern of type *b'*.

It is obvious that when *c* and *c'* and *b* and *b'* are equivalent, then formulizations A and B describe exactly the same general situation. The primary concern of the scientist (after classifying objects according to their characteristics) is to describe the regularities of behavior exhibited in nature. This is done adequately with formulization A, and it is to A that we refer when we speak below of scientific laws or lawlike generalizations. We do not talk in terms of cause and effect because we wish to avoid the technical difficulties involved in attempts to distinguish between so-called causal and accidental regularities in nature. Our discussion in terms of formulization A can easily be translated into terms of formulization B, thus generating these technical problems, but for practical purposes of explanation and prediction, scientific laws can usually be expressed in terms of lawlike generalizations descriptive of natural regularities quite adequately without a discussion of cause and effect. That is, if a lawlike generalization is confirmed in experience, it can be useful for prediction—if not for explanation—even if the regularity it describes is thought to be "accidental." And if an accidental regularity does submit to description in terms of a confirmable lawlike generalization, then it probably can be made satisfactory as an explanation if one explains it in terms of another "causal" regularity.

A scientific theory consists of a set of statements descriptive of the various types of objects under study with respect to their characteristics and a set of lawlike generalizations descriptive of the behavior of objects of these types in various circumstances. To explain the behavior of any particular object, one subsumes it under the general law that describes the general circumstances, objects, and behavior of which the particular circumstances, object, and behavior are exemplifications. If one knows only the particular object and its behavior, one can use the general law as a guide in searching for the particular circumstances involved. If one knows only the particular circumstances and object, one can use the general law as a guide in searching for the particular behavior that will ensue in this particular case. In scientific explanation, then, the behavior of a particular is explained by giving the lawlike generalization of which the particular and its circumstances are an instance. In scientific prediction, the behavior of a particular is predicted with reference to the lawlike generalization of which the particular and its circumstances are an instance.

The basic laws of a scientific theory are generalizations based on experience. An ideal of scientific enquiry is to organize the laws that make up a scientific theory so that some of them are axioms from which the others—theorems—can be deduced by logical methods. Using these axioms, it is also possible to deduce theorems that are not included in the original set of laws. These new theorems are in the form of lawlike generalizations that can be interpreted as describing the behavior of objects in the field of inquiry. They can be postulated as laws, but before they are accepted as such they must be tested by observation and experiment. The great value of *axiomatization* for scientists is that it provides a powerful method for suggesting possible laws about natural regularities that might not be noticed in ordinary experience. Axiomatization thus provides a new level of explanation and prediction. General scientific laws themselves can be explained with reference to the axioms from which they can be deduced as theorems, and new laws can be predicted in the form of new theorems deduced from the established laws taken as axioms. However, these laws must be descriptive of the regularities exhibited by the behavior of particular objects in the world if the theory is to provide scientific knowledge and understanding of the world. If a theorem is deduced that describes a regularity not found in nature, then the proposed law may simply be rejected, or another axiomatization of the basic laws tried, or a check may be made to see if one or more of the basic laws might itself be unconfirmable for some reason previously overlooked. For single lawlike generalizations, one contradictory case may be enough to lead to the rejection of the law. But for scientific theories as a whole, the deduction of a theorem that, when proposed as a law, is contradicted by experience may lead to the rejection of the proposed law, but not to the rejection of the complete scientific theory. Lawlike generalizations clearly lose a great deal of value when there are real exceptions to them, but it is not clear that axiomatizations of scientific theories lose their value if some theorems deduced from them are not descriptive of regularities in the natural world. This is to say we agree that single laws must "fit" the world to be used for explanation and prediction, but that axiomatized scientific theories need not do so completely and exactly, at least in practice, to have explanatory and predictive value.

It is often said that the social sciences, and in particular anthropology, are still in the data-collecting stage, with social scientists busily describing and classifying their objects of study but formulating no laws about them. It is even claimed by some that it is not the business of social scientists, and particularly not that of anthropologists, to formulate scientific laws, either because of some dogmatic opinion about the goals of the social sciences or because of a mistaken belief that the social sciences are not "sciences" in the same sense as the physical sciences. Taking anthropology as an example, however, it is not true that anthropologists have not yet reached the stage of formulating laws of human behavior. In Chapter 3 we begin our description of various ways of life on the foundation of three basic laws of animal survival that could well be considered axioms. In psychology, sociology, and anthropology there are thousands of lawlike generalizations that are confirmably descriptive of regularities of human behavior. Most of these are unfairly denigrated (even by social scientists themselves) as "truisms" that do not merit the dignity of being called laws. The principal difficulty with the lawlike generalizations that make up "folk wisdom" and to which we appeal for guidance in our everyday interactions with one another is not that they are not confirmable, but that so many of them have either very wide or very narrow application. Limited lawlike generalizations are good as far as they go, but often the required circumstances, even when described in general terms, are very rarely exactly duplicated in experience. And widely applicable laws of human behavior tend to be very general indeed. It is certainly true, for example, that if a man is not specially conditioned to behave otherwise, he will become angry if he is annoyed beyond a certain degree. But if a person wants to specify what sorts of things annoy man and what degree of annoyance is required to elicit anger, he finds it very difficult to generalize. He may be able to give explicit generalizations for particular men (the mere sound of a radio anytime and anywhere will annoy Alan and make him angry) or for particular groups of men (French men are annoyed and angered by American women), but here the circumstances will have to exclude conditions that might alter these attitudes. Lawlike generalizations of this sort can very well be descriptive of actual regularities of human behavior, but they may be so restricted in circumstances and applicability as to be of quite limited value in explanation and prediction. Their value is limited not because they are inaccurate descriptions of regularities, but because they generalize over such limited domains of objects and because it is very difficult to determine, given the number of explicit circumstances that must be taken into consideration, whether a given situation is an exemplification of the general law.

It is the difficulty of formulating, confirming, and applying laws in the social sciences that has led some people to the mistaken conclusion that the social sciences are different from the physical sciences. It has been claimed, for example, that there can be no laws with which we can explain or predict human behavior because the historical sequence of human affairs consists of unique events brought about by the particular actions of individual men. It is true that every man and every human action is unique, but so is every particular ounce of sulfur and every individual chemical reaction. But because the behavior of one ounce of sulfur is very much like the behavior of any other ounce of sulfur, whereas the behavior of one man is very often quite different from the behavior of other men (and the behavior of men much more various and complex than the behavior of ounces of sulfur), some people are led to believe that physics is much more "scientific" than anthropology. Actually, laws are just more difficult to formulate, confirm, and apply in anthropology because the objects of study are much more rare and complex and their behavior is more difficult to understand.

For example, if an ounce of sulfur is burned in air, some of the sulfur combines with hydrogen to form the compound H_2S. A general law can be written describing this chemical reaction. Sulfur is commonly available, the circumstances are easy to duplicate, the reaction takes a very short time, and so the law can be confirmed readily by observation and experiment. It is also relatively easy to determine that the substance is sulfur and that the particular circumstances are instances of those described in the general law. Because many of the objects and events studied in physical sciences are as simple as those we have just described, there is a large body of physical laws confirmed to a high degree of probability.

On the other hand, consider the evolution of a set of culture traits throughout history in a particular society. The circumstances are extremely complex and difficult to discern completely, the culture traits have subtle characteristics and are difficult to describe, and the behavior of the objects being studied is exhibited in a complex event extended over wide stretches of space and time. Furthermore, on earth there are no known instances of other complex events similar enough to be classified as a type with the one being studied. In human history there are, of course, many examples of the evolution of culture traits in a society, but this category is too general—or so it is sometimes claimed—to be of much help in explaining the particular evolution of culture traits in a particular society; and laws on such a level of generality are said to be of no help at all in predicting the particular future evolutionary course of culture traits in a particular society. The same sort of claim is sometimes made about the evolution of *Homo sapiens*—that there are no general laws that can be used to explain the particular course of the past history of this complex event or to predict the particularities of its ongoing course in the future.

If a person believes that man and his culture are parts of nature and thus can be explained scientifically as can the rest of nature (assumptions necessary to scientific anthropology), then he must admit that confirmable laws—laws that explain human evolution, for example—can be formulated, whether he knows them or not. It is, in fact, the human condition and perhaps the rarity of the objects and events studied in anthropology that limit man's knowledge of anthropological laws. In the first place, man's intellect may not be adequate to the comprehension and understanding of the highly complex objects and events he studies in anthropology. And even if he might be capable of understanding were he to gain enough familiarity with these objects and events, they are spread so widely in space and time that no man can hope to observe them adequately. No man was present to observe the early stages of the evolution of *Homo sapiens*, and no man lives long enough to observe the evolution of a culture trait over the centuries in a particular society. Beyond this, the nature and the magnitude of anthropological objects and events rule out the possibility of man's duplicating such situations in an experiment as he can easily with the sulfur reaction described above. Finally, it may very well be the case that in our universe *Homo sapiens*, for example, has evolved only once, so that it would be impossible for any being to observe several instances of this type of event. It is easier to formulate laws in the physical sciences than in the social sciences because the objects and events of the physical sciences are more easily understood by man, of such magnitude in time and space as to be easily observed and manipulated in an experiment, and of such quantities that man can observe many examples of each type. That this is not the case for many objects and events of the social sciences does not mean that no laws that explain these events can be formulated; it means simply that man may not be capable of deriving these laws with his limited intellect on the basis of inadequate observations of a single available instance, often the only one that exists.

We believe, however, that the prospects for the derivation of scientific laws in anthropology are not so dismal as the discussion above might lead one to believe. One of the most important aspects of human knowledge is that it is cumulative: it is transmitted by cultural means from generation to generation. What one man may not be able to comprehend or observe, a succession of men may investigate piecemeal until finally one man absorbs the accumulated data and finds himself capable of formulating laws.

It is sometimes claimed that an event in the social sciences can be explained by looking at the circumstances that led up to it, whereas no examination of the circumstances prior to the event would be sufficient to allow one to predict it. In concluding this short essay in the philosophy of science, we must point out that we have assumed the parity of explanation and prediction. That is, we have assumed that whatever can be explained by subsumption under a set of lawlike generalizations can also be predicted with reference to that same set. It is a mistake—the result of confusing empirical with logical matters—to contend that what can be explained after an event has occurred could not logically have been predicted prior to the occurrence of the event. It may be the case in a given situation that by examining the circumstances, men can derive laws that explain the event only after the event has occurred and they have seen what it is. This would appear to be usual even in the simplest cases of physical science. Men may not have capacities of intellect great enough to derive from the circumstances alone laws sufficient for the prediction of the event that is bound to occur. This is an empirical matter of man's intellectual capacities. It is also often the case that no man could have predicted the event, such as the evolution of *Homo sapiens*, because no man was present prior to the event to make the prediction. But these empirical matters of man's intellectual capacity and his existence in time should not be allowed to confuse a logical issue. When regularities exist—whether any man has derived laws about them—then events that result from situations that exemplify possible laws could be explained and predicted with reference to these laws, if they were formulated. The parity of explanation and prediction is, then, a matter of logic.

It is now possible to consider the present book within the structure of science as we describe it. This is a work of analysis and synthesis. We do not present new data, nor do we give summary reports. The chapters that follow, therefore, are not on the first order of scientific inquiry because they are not directly descriptive of the characteristics and behavior of actual objects of anthropological study. The ways of life we describe—of the nonhuman primate, the protohuman, and the various stages of man—are instead *abstract constructions*, based on the most reliable facts available; consequently, we are engaged in pursuing the second and third orders of scientific business. We benefit from the data of anthropology, collected for over one hundred years, by examining these data to isolate principles that can be expressed (although we do not often put them this way) in the form of lawlike generalizations of formulization A, and to discover the most typical structure of each way of life. Then we organize these principles logically in a quasi-axiomatic fashion, proceeding from the more basic to the less basic in each way of life. Next—and always with the aid of the facts about real societies as they are now known—we elaborate these principles, show the logical relations among them, and allude to the quasi-deduction of principles and features that they allow. The results of this procedure are hypothetical constructions descriptive of possible ways of life, based explicitly on known anthropological facts and on analyses of the logical relations among the principles and elements of each way of life.

We do not put many of the principles we isolate in the form of lawlike generalizations for two reasons. First, we are quite aware of their tentativeness, and so we are informal in order to avoid, if possible, the stigma of dogmatism. Second, to make such lawlike generalizations reasonably acceptable, the circumstances for each would have to be specified to a degree that would not enhance the basic points we wish to make and that in many cases could not be done because too little is known about the circumstances. We do, however, state three laws of animal survival based on the requirement of all animals for protection, nutrition, and reproduction. These laws are the basis for our analyses and syntheses throughout Chapters 3–10. The principles we isolate are also cumulative throughout these chapters. The principles stressed in the chapters on the ways of life of the protohuman and elemental man, for example, are foundations for the structure of the ways of life discussed in later chapters, although they may not be discussed in great detail there. The basic and essential elements are treated most completely where they first become important.

The overall development of Chapters 3–10 is based on the principle of proceeding from simple to complex. The ways of life are categorized according to a step-by-step increase in complexity, based on increasing degrees of intelligence of the nonhuman, protohuman, and human primates. Human ways of life are differentiated by man's increasingly complex cultural means of coping with the physical environment. Within each chapter, the more basic principles are discussed first and in most detail; other elements of the particular way of life are often shown to relate directly to the structural elaboration of the first principles. For example, in analyzing the nonhuman primate way of life, we find that much can be explained with reference to the way nonhuman primates satisfy their requirement for protection. But when we begin to discuss the way of life of advanced hunters and gatherers, we find that the problems of protection have been largely met and therefore do not require much discussion; instead, in that chapter we discuss in some detail specialized solutions to the problem of procuring food. In later chapters, we examine increasingly complex ways of using nonhuman sources of energy. In the final "way of life" chapter we find that the most serious problems facing atomic man stem from the quantitatively extravagant way he satisfies the requirement to reproduce.

The basic orientation of this study is ecological. Man must be a balanced part of nature if he is to survive on earth. Each of the ways of life we describe for man constitutes a way of interacting with the physical environment to satisfy basic animal requirements. Underlying the most esoteric of cultural needs are the basic requirements of the individual to protect himself, to nourish himself, and to reproduce himself if the species is to survive. No matter how ingenious man's cultural methods of utilizing the physical environment to satisfy his needs, he cannot be successful in the end if they lead to the disruption of the ecological community of which he is the dominant animal member. It is, therefore, alarming that the ways of life of industrial and atomic man show an ecological imbalance between man and nature.

We stress the synthetic, hypothetical, abstract, constructive nature of the eight descriptions of ways of life in the chapters that follow. However, they differ from the constructions anthropologists give as descriptive of societies they study in the field only in being more general. That they are abstractions, not factual summaries, should not detract from their value as serious attempts to present what is essential in the eight ways of life discussed. The simplification and organization of principles and elements along logical lines is for the purpose of understanding.

It is our conviction that scientific progress is made primarily through the posing and testing of hypotheses. The following syntheses are presented, therefore, as working hypotheses to aid in the investigation of a number of ways of life. They exhibit the basic elements, principles, and logical relations essential to the understanding of man's interaction with nature.

2 DEFINITIONS: MAN, CULTURE, AND NATURE

Man is part of nature. His culture, however, is apart from nature. Whatever man does or produces is at once natural and cultural. By contrasting man and his culture with the rest of nature, we can describe and understand man's place in the natural world. To make this contrast, we must know what we mean when we speak of man and his culture. Man is an animal of the mammalian class, of the primate order, and of the genus and species *Homo sapiens,* or rational man. Culture consists of all man's activities and products. Nature is, in the broadest sense, the entire world—all its processes and contents, including man and culture. If we exclude man, nature is the physical environment, which here includes the nonhuman biological environment—everything in the world except man and culture.

These general definitions enable us to begin a meaningful contrast between man and nature. Let us first sketch briefly the general characteristics of the mammal. What basic sort of animal is man? Next we shall describe abstractly the two environments with which man interacts—the physical and the cultural. How do they differ, interact, and overlap? The brief characterizations of physical and cultural environments given below are abstractions that emphasize the structural foundations underlying all environmental elaborations, whatever the particular circumstances. With this information, we proceed in Chapters 3–10 with a detailed description and analysis of the ways of life of the nonhuman primate, of the protohuman, and of man.

The mammal is a vertebrate chordate, an animal with a backbone protecting a spinal nerve cord, which is an essential integrating and conducting part of the synaptic nervous system. Chordates have definite front-rear orientation and are bilaterally symmetrical, which means that their right and left sides are, roughly, mirror images. At the front end of the spinal cord, most chordates have a large concentration of neural tissue—the brain. In the brain an associational system integrates two parts of the central nervous system: the sensory, which carries stimuli from the sense organs, and the motor, which effects muscular reactions to stimuli. The multiplicity of synapses allows for varied stimuli and responses. Brain size and complexity become greater with the increase of associational capacity (intelligence), sensory discrimination, and motor dexterity. A fundamental characteristic of most mammals is their constant body temperature, which accounts for their so-called warm-bloodedness. They have three basic skin specializations: hair, sweat glands, and sebaceous glands. Fertilization is internal, and the young of almost all mammals are born live. Mammary glands are the essential distinguishing feature of mammals; in the females these glands produce milk for feeding the young immediately after their birth. The order of terrestrial mammals with the most highly developed neural organization is the primate order, and the most complex primate is man.

The physical environment consists of the earth—its rocks, soil, surface waters, and atmosphere; its weather and climate; and its plant and animal life, including man—and all the forces and processes, including solar radiation, that integrate the elements of the earth into a worldwide thermodynamic system. According to the second law of thermodynamics, the forces of the universe are moving toward complete expenditure of energy, at which point, theoretically, matter will be in a state of complete rest, and the temperature of everything will be absolute zero. On earth, a temporary counterforce appears to exist in living things. All the energy of life on earth comes ultimately from energy radiated by the sun, first captured by green plants during the process of photosynthesis. The life of plants, animals that eat plants, and animals that eat animals depends on solar energy. No animal is self-sufficient; if all plants on earth were to die, soon all animals would die as well. And for photosynthesis, plants depend not only on solar radiation but also on soil, water, and the atmosphere.

The physical conditions necessary to the growth of plants result from the actions of certain forces on the matter of the earth—actions initiated and sustained primarily by the force of gravitation. Every particle in the universe attracts every other particle with a force directly proportional to their masses and inversely proportional to the square of the distance between them. This force holds the earth together, rotates it on its axis, propels it around the sun, and thus generates day and night, the seasons, and the world's climates and weather. The force of gravitation accounts for the rise of mountain chains and the formation of ocean basins and for the erosion of the earth by wind and water. Its laws are fundamental to the release of heat, chemical, electrical, and atomic energy. Plant life and thus all life on earth depends, therefore, as much on the force of gravitation as on solar radiation.

The earth as a whole can be considered as a system in dynamic equilibrium, where natural forces, acting in harmony, contribute to the conservation of matter and energy. If we take the earth as a complete system and consider the radiant energy received from the sun as a constant, we can say that virtually no matter or energy is gained or lost on earth. Subsystems of matter and energy on earth can also be considered to be in dynamic equilibrium. The thermodynamic systems of chief interest to us are ecological communities, defined in terms of natural geographic areas and the life forms that inhabit them. An example is a pond with a constant supply of water in which the species and numbers of individuals are delicately balanced with one another and with the perennially constant environment. In an ecological system, the number of living species and of individuals of each species may vary, but the total energy exchange and matter content remain constant. Ideal equilibrium is reached when (1) the number and kinds of species do not vary, (2) the number of individuals of each species varies interdependently around established norms, (3) climatic conditions provide repetitive sequences of seasons and weather, and (4) the waste products of living things, combined with the weathering of rocks, provide constantly fertile soil conditions. On earth, conditions promoting this ideal equilibrium in a particular ecological community prevail only for relatively short periods of time—a few years, a few centuries, or perhaps a few millennia. But even in unbalanced systems, the energy exchanges can be seen as modifications of the system that will lead to conditions under which a dynamic equilibrium can be maintained. If a pond fills with plants, for example, it may change slowly into a peat bog, with new life forms in ecological balance.

Mammals, primates, and men are all members of ecological communities. Their actions thus constitute part of the energy exchange and contribute to the continuation or disruption of dynamic equilibrium. Man's physical environment, that is, nature excluding man, consists of the total ecological community—its physical features and its living inhabitants—in which man lives and with which he interacts. Again, in such a system the quantity of matter and energy remains constant despite dynamic interaction. The importance of this for humans is that in an ecological system (the earth as a whole, for example), matter and energy resources are finite. In most ecological systems the actions of members of one species can often be seen to dominate the form of the dynamic balance of the whole. Man has steadily increased his influence on the physical environment, dominating the ecological community of the earth and thus controlling the form of the earth's dynamic ecological balance.

Man has altered his position in the earth's ecological community by gaining more and more control over the physical environment through his creation of culture. Among the products with which man directs, modifies, and controls the physical environment are fire, tools, and social institutions that regulate conduct. All cultural accomplishments depend on the use of symbolic language, man's major cultural product. Since only men have language, only men have culture, and only men live in a cultural environment. From the viewpoint of nonhuman living things, however, man's products are not cultural but natural parts of the physical environment.

The products of man's activity are, therefore, part of both the cultural and the physical environment at the same time. In their physical manifestations, these cultural products are certainly part of the physical environment, subject to the laws of nature. It is their direct or indirect production according to man's intentions that makes them part of the cultural environment as well. Since man is a part of nature and since he acts upon and modifies the natural physical environment, he produces a natural result. But for the purposes of indicating that he proceeds with artifice, we call his results artificial and the products he has made and the environment he has modified cultural.

Language, on which the creation of culture depends, is a form of symbolic behavior. Like men, nonhuman primates have systems of social relations; they use tools to a limited extent and modify the physical environment. However, they do not have a culture and do not create a cultural environment because none of their actions or products are symbolic. That is, they communicate to a large degree not intentionally but incidentally by way of natural signs that express their emotional states. Without the intentional use of symbols, nonhuman primates can have no language, and without language there can be no culture. The key for determining whether a primate is a man is the distinction between incidental communication by means of signs and intentional communication by means of symbols.

II | WAYS OF LIFE

A | *Control by Nature*

3 | THE NONHUMAN PRIMATE

Animals must solve three problems to survive. These requirements are so basic that they can be written as laws. In logical order, to survive in the environment of the earth an animal must act:

1. to protect himself,
2. to nourish himself, and
3. to reproduce himself.

The first two are essential to the preservation of the individual, and all three, to the preservation of the species. That is, some individuals must be secure and nurtured if they are to reproduce so the species can survive.

Among mammals, as among other animals, the anatomy and physiology of the organism contribute greatly to the satisfaction of these requirements. For example, the skin and hair form a protective covering; various internal defensive and regulatory mechanisms automatically fend off harm and stimulate the search for food and water, on which growth and preservation of life depend. Sexual activity, on which procreation depends, is also regulated internally. Anatomical and physiological differences between species can be seen functionally as different mechanisms for solving the basic problems.

Among living nonhuman primates, those that resemble man most closely anatomically, physiologically, and behaviorally are the baboons, chimpanzees, gorillas, and macaques. On the basis of their characteristics, we can construct the ideal (i.e., imagined, not actual) nonhuman primate, the animal most closely related to man but still an animal. We select these "manlike" primates for the synthesis of our generalized nonhuman primate and his way of life, explicitly excluding from consideration in our construction prosimians, arboreal monkeys, and all other groups of primates. We do not provide an exact description of any one group, but a model that helps us to understand the ways of life of actual nonhuman primate groups. This hypothetical model of the nonhuman primate is thus a product of two courses of inference. Inductively, from current factual knowledge, we construct a generalized model of nonhuman primate anatomy, physiology, and behavior. In cases where we must choose between conflicting characteristics, of gorillas and baboons, for example, we make the model more like the baboon, as the way of life of the baboon is more like that of elemental man. Deductively, by logical analysis, we derive more detailed features from the generalized model in conjunction with the three basic laws of animal survival. The deduction of anatomical and physiological features is important in the next chapter, where we construct the protohuman.

With such a model in mind, we can take the first step toward determining the features that distinguish man from the nonhuman primates (and thus from all other animals): distinguishing the nonhuman primate from other mammals.

The most obvious anatomical characteristic distinguishing the model nonhuman primate from most other mammals is the position of the head. The heads of most other mammals are positioned to face in a direction parallel to the line of the spinal column, with the nose foremost. This allows an animal standing on all fours to look around horizontally. The bear, like many other mammals, can stand on his hind legs or sit upright and in these positions bend his head down so that it faces in a direction that makes a right angle with his spine; but his usual body position is horizontal on four legs. The head of the nonhuman primate, on the other hand, is positioned so that it naturally points in a direction that makes a right angle with the spinal column. When the nonhuman primate stands upright on two legs, his body points vertically upward, but his head faces forward on a horizontal plane. When he drops on all fours, he must lift his head up in order to look forward.

The front and rear limbs of the nonhuman primate are clearly differentiated into legs and arms; the arms are longer than the legs. His hip girdle is oriented so that he can walk readily and, with even more agility, run on two legs, although the normal form of ground locomotion for the nonhuman primate is on all fours. When he stands upright or sits, his arms swing free. His hand is unique in that it has a fully rotatable thumb that can meet the four fingers in at least partial opposition, allowing him not only to grasp large objects firmly with the whole hand but also to manipulate small objects between the thumb and fingers. He can examine these objects with stereoscopic color vision.

Nonhuman primates are sexually dimorphic, an anatomical characteristic expressed in the larger body and larger canine teeth of the males. The average male weighs around 150 pounds; females can weigh as little as 75 pounds. Both sexes have an average life span of twenty years; they are capable of reproduction at about the age of five or six and are fully mature at eight.

Females have periods of estrus throughout the year, during which they are fertile and sexually receptive and actively seek out males for copulation. Unlike other mammals, sexual intercourse may occur among most nonhuman primates at any time, although nonhuman primate males do not usually seek to copulate except with females in estrus. Births are ordinarily single. The newborn has some ability to cling to his mother, but she must regularly support him with her hand for the first few days. After being weaned, the nonhuman primate is omnivorous, although his diet is usually about 80 percent vegetable; animal protein generally comes from such things as grubs, bird eggs, and small animals.

The amount of neural tissue in the brain, and especially the size of the cerebral cortex, is very large, both in absolute terms and in terms of body size. The result is greater intelligence than most other mammals, heightened powers of perceptual integration, greater dexterity and motor control, and thus greater facility in problem solving.

A nonhuman primate of this general anatomical and physiological constitution can adapt to a wide range of tropical and temperate environments. The absolute limits of his geographic distribution are set by temperature; his hair covering and metabolism are not adequate to protect him in climates where the daytime temperature regularly drops to 32 degrees Fahrenheit or lower, nor can he withstand temperatures regularly exceeding 120 degrees Fahrenheit. Within these extremes, the presence and numbers of nonhuman primates are theoretically limited by the amount of accessible food and water and by their ability to protect themselves from environmental hazards. In a situation that affords an abundance of food and water and maximum protection, the total number of nonhuman primates in a given area is actually determined by natural social relations within groups and between groups. Even in the best of circumstances, a group seldom exceeds one or two hundred members and seldom ranges over less than two or three square miles or more than fifteen.

Let us now consider the behavior of a model group of ordinarily terrestrial nonhuman primates as they solve the problems raised by the basic requirements for protection, nutrition, and reproduction. The primary step in protection is the formation of the group itself. Infants are necessarily dependent upon their mothers for protection for several months after birth; this dependence is the initial form of social contact. But even an adult nonhuman primate is poorly equipped to protect himself alone. He must cluster together with others for warmth, and although he has strong jaws and sharp teeth, they are inadequate against such predators as big cats. He can run as fast as twenty miles per hour for a few hundred feet, but so can cats. Furthermore, when alone he cannot keep alert at all times, watching for danger. The fact that the lone individual soon loses his life to the hazards of the physical environment because he cannot protect himself adequately is repeatedly demonstrated by the fate of nonhuman primates who are separated from the group because of sickness, getting lost, or being expelled. A group provides protection in the form of numbers. A predator attacks a group of defensive nonhuman primates much more cautiously than he attacks a lone animal, if he attacks at all. In a group there are always some members who notice imminent danger; their cries as they flee warn others in time for them to run for trees or other protection. Because of their need for protection, nonhuman primates are animals that live in groups. Otherwise, survival in the physical environment would be very unlikely.

The activity of the nonhuman primate to satisfy his basic requirements creates other problems. Individuals must not only protect themselves from outside dangers; within a group they must protect themselves from one another. This is accomplished through the establishment and recognition of dominance relations among the individuals of the group. Dominance is most strongly expressed among males; in battle or, more often, through threatening behavior that forces a challenger to back down, each male attains his place. Each individual learns or establishes his place and defers to those above him. His place is not simply one of rank; definite physical distances are maintained between individuals at different levels. Once dominance patterns are established, internal conflict is rare except when a strong young adult challenges an old male of failing powers. Squabbles among adolescents or females are almost always stopped by dominant males, who either actively intervene or accept the role of protector when a persecuted animal runs to them for refuge. Weaker dominance patterns exist among the females. The female's place is more variable than the male's as a result of her sexual roles. When in estrus she may share the dominance position of the male with whom she consorts, thus assuming a place within the dominance pattern of the males; while nursing she takes a position of comfortable subordinance to the males in the group. Mothers with young have control of their young and dominance over females without young.

If the climate is such that protection is sometimes needed from the weather or from low night temperatures, the group must find shelter. They are most likely to seek it within their territory, to which they return at night if they have traveled outside it during the day. They may make nests for comfort or for warmth, but they establish no permanent home base within the territory. This means that the members of the group must always stay together, for there is no specific place to which the group returns each night where a separated member might go with assurance of finding his fellows. All the imperatives following from the primary requirement for protection lead to the necessity for constant group coherence. Our model nonhuman primates are, by necessity, group-living animals. Because each group must protect its territory, the simple principles of dominance often apply also between groups. Direct conflict between groups seldom occurs. If two groups meet and cannot ignore one another, they threaten one another until one backs off or until they reach an impasse and drift apart.

What is most striking about the overall dominance pattern is the way it formalizes individual aggression within the group. An explicit program for establishing the place of each individual in a scale of dominance enables each to protect himself from the others in his group by keeping to his place and therefore makes the group as a whole cohesive. The dominance arrangement of the group does create a slight amount of anxiety in each individual. If he is dominant he expects deference, and if he is subordinate he must be ready to pay deference. In either case, the tension is never equal to that between animals that have no defined positions and may actually fight. But the tension is present whenever the nonhuman primate is reminded of his place in society. Overriding this social tension, however, is the great satisfaction in being a member of the group. Within the group an individual is safe; knowing his place and how he must behave removes uncertainties, and by being among his own kind, an individual has the comfort of mutual activity and company. Nonhuman primates groom one another in many different situations but most often when the group is calm, well fed, and protected. Subordinates groom dominant males, consorts groom each other, mothers groom their young, and near peers groom each other. The social contact gives both groomer and groomed great satisfaction—satisfaction that is derived from the comfort they feel as members of the group. This satisfaction is not, however, the basic factor that holds the group together. No individual could *survive* alone; therefore, it is because of the requirement for protection in the broadest sense that nonhuman primates live in groups.

The second basic requirement is for food and water. The simplest solution here is for each individual of the group to forage for himself. From the time he is weaned, each nonhuman primate is a complete economic unit, gathering all and only the food he himself consumes, seldom sharing what he collects with other individuals.

When each individual collects his own food, problems arise as to which individuals get the choice selections. The principles of dominance settle these problems at once; dominant individuals always have first choice over subordinates. The economic independence of each individual and dominance behavior provide logical reasons for the fact that nonhuman primates seldom carry or store food: an individual cannot protect what he does not consume on the spot; if he attempts to carry food, a dominant male will soon take it, and if he stores food, other alert individuals will be likely to find and take it. In addition, it is physically difficult for a nonhuman primate to carry anything for very long. Finally, most of his staples are perishable.

The group as a whole must ensure a perpetual and adequate food and water supply for each of its members. This is accomplished by establishing a range large enough to provide nutritive necessities, over which it can roam either daily or throughout the year. A group's range usually contains more resources than are needed to satisfy its food needs so that separate groups meeting on the fringes of overlapping ranges do not come into conflict. But the need to ensure a minimally adequate area for food collection leads to the establishment of central territory within the range that must be protected against other groups. Consequently, conflict between groups is most likely to occur when one group encroaches on another's central territory.

The social problems resulting from the requirement to reproduce are solved by threat or force. A female in estrus is activated physiologically to solicit among the males, and whichever is the more dominant among those desiring to copulate wins the right to mate with her. The male has no special role in caring for his offspring. Infants are raised by their mothers, and the interest taken in them by the fathers does not greatly exceed the general protective concern males exhibit for any member of the group.

It has been suggested that sexual ties account for the cohesiveness of the group, but in our analysis sexual matters necessarily come after action has been taken to ensure self-protection and to secure food and water. The nonhuman primate seldom if ever becomes so engrossed with his desire to copulate that he fails to seek protection in case of danger.

That mutual protection rather than sexual ties is the binding factor in nonhuman primate groups is clear from the persistence of the group in two possibly disruptive sexual situations. If sexual matters were of prime importance to the individual, he could not practice the restraint necessary for keeping order within the group. In large groups it is possible that there will always be some females in estrus. Far from meaning that sexually receptive females are available to all the males all the time, this means that most of the males have to practice restraint in the face of sexual provocation most of the time, since the dominant males monopolize the females in estrus. They can override the tensions and antagonisms aroused by such sexual privation and remain as orderly members of the group because the protection afforded by the group is more important to them than is copulation. An alternate possibility not uncommon among nonhuman primate groups is a situation in which none of the females is in estrus. Here, too, it is obviously the need for protection that holds the group together.

If individuals are to live successfully integrated lives in a group, they must have a workable system of communication. The simplest such system for nonhuman primates is one in which every individual sees the direct responsive actions of every other individual to the environment. According to his physical and social position, each individual can then respond appropriately in harmony to the actions of the others. Complete visual monitoring of the behavior of others is impossible in large groups and is not always possible in small groups. But nonhuman primates, and other animals as well, are able to make various vocal responses that occur distinctively in different circumstances and that are accompanied by different action responses. A specific vocalization always accompanies a specific, direct, responsive action. The vocalization can be interpreted by another individual, therefore, as a *sign* of how the vocalizer is feeling or of what he is doing or experiencing. It is important to note that the vocalization is a natural response to the situation and that it is not *intended* by the vocalizer as a sign. The individual who hears the vocalization can interpret it as a sign, but there is no intent on the part of the vocalizer to send a message. He does not mean to communicate; he is simply conditioned by nature and circumstances to make varying noises in different situations. Thus, communication among nonhuman primates occurs when one individual takes certain aspects of another's behavior as signs of what that individual is experiencing.

This system of communication is a natural outgrowth of the way nonhuman primates perceive and respond to the physical environment. In forming his perception, the individual discriminates among various aspects of the environment. Instinctively and through experience he associates different perceptions with actual and possible experiences. In most circumstances his behavior can be seen as an immediate and appropriate response to the environmental situation as he perceives it and when he is not restrained from acting: if there is danger, he seeks protection; if he is hungry, he seeks food and eats it when he finds it; if he is attracted to a female in estrus, he copulates.

Individuals must learn to perceive things through the various senses. Infants at play and adults seeking to satisfy their curiosity are both exploring their environment and learning the distinguishing perceptible characteristics of such important features of the environment as danger, food, and other nonhuman primates. Once an individual learns some of the characteristics, he can begin to take certain of his perceptions as signs of environmental circumstances more extensive than the immediate situation he has actually perceived. A nonhuman primate may respond to the sound of a breaking twig by grimacing, shrieking, dropping the food he is eating, and running to climb the nearest tree. He does this not out of fear of broken twigs, but because he takes the sound of a breaking twig as a sign of the approach of a predator. What is significant here is that the predator does not intend the sound to be a sign of his approach, but the nonhuman primate can and does take it as a sign, just as he may take a sweet odor as a sign of food or the shriek of a companion as a sign of danger. The physical world does not send messages to an individual, but individuals who are familiar with the world's characteristics can take many of their perceptions as signs of environmental conditions beyond those immediate perceptions.

The activity of the nonhuman primate is his direct response to his perception of the environment. This response is appropriate behavior, given the animal's immediate needs and the environmental situation as he perceives it. Among nonhuman primates, besides the primary response of direct action, there are secondary responses—facial expressions, bodily postures, and vocalizations—that can be taken as expressing the individual's emotional state. These secondary responses, although partially learned, are largely inherited. Each different general situation evokes specific facial, bodily, and vocal secondary responses. These responses are always made in the presence of the stimulus and accompany appropriate action. Other animals can therefore take the secondary response as a natural sign of the presence of the stimulus—a predator, food, a female in estrus, and so on. What is to be stressed is that such facial, bodily, and vocal behavior is a natural response to a stimulus, coextensive with, although secondary to, direct coping action. Animals learn to interpret their perceptions of such behavior in others through a combination of sympathetic response and conditioning by experience. They have the same secondary responses in similar situations; therefore, when they hear a certain shriek, for example, they are reminded of the associated primary response, the activity they would perform were they to make such a shriek. And so they immediately run for protection or at least look around for danger. An animal can and does respond, of course, to the primary responses of other animals, running when they do, hiding when they hide, and so on.

Bodily actions, bodily postures, and facial expressions must be seen to be taken as signs, but in a group of primates, every animal cannot be in the line of vision of every other animal. Thus, a system of communication that depends on visual signs alone is clearly unsatisfactory. The most important channel of communication among all primates, including man, is the vocal-auditory. According to the laws of physics, sound waves spread out from their source in a series of concentric circles, losing energy as they travel farther from the sound source. The nonhuman primate can project his vocalization so that it is louder along one directional line. Thus, though he sends his sound in all directions, his vocalization is received most clearly from the direction he is facing. The dual auditory organs of the non-

human primate are correspondingly suited to both the general re-
ception of sound and the directional location of its source. The nonhuman primate learns to turn his head so that the sound is balanced
at its loudest in each ear; usually he is then facing its source. Since
sounds fade rapidly, many different vocalizations from different
directions can be discriminated in a short period of time. The most
important advantage of the vocal-auditory channel over the visual
channel, however, is that sounds can travel around and through
many objects that obscure sight. An animal can hear, and take as a
sign of danger, the vocalization of another animal he cannot see.

Communication between nonhuman primates is based on one
individual's use of another's perceptions and responses. Nonhuman
primates take the actions, expressions, and especially sounds of
others as signs of data about their environment. There is, however,
little if any evidence that they intentionally signal one another;
hence, their communication does not constitute the use of language,
which by definition involves the *intentional* transmittal of messages.
A nonhuman primate may respond identically to each of these signs
of danger: the sight of a leopard, the sound of a breaking twig or of
a shriek, and the sight of another individual running toward a tree,
making a certain facial expression, or assuming a certain bodily
posture.

In summary, nonhuman primates do not use language; they take
the behavior of other individuals as signs, but they do not intend
their responses to be taken as signs by others. Communication
among nonhuman primates is logically a special case of inherited
and learned responses to perceptible stimuli from the physical environment. So-called animal calls, warning signals, lullings of infants,
and so on are not really forms of intentional communication. It is
our tendency to anthropomorphize that leads us to refer to them as
calls.

Nonhuman primates have a large repertory of vocalizations for
different situations. They can be classified in various ways, most
simply according to pain and pleasure. Vocalizations of pain include

those of fright, tension, territorial possession, dominance position, and annoyance, as well as special vocalizations for danger. Among vocalizations of pleasure are those of the discovery and consumption of food, of sexual and maternal satisfaction, of social comfort, and of friendly relations. About twenty different vocalizations for twenty different general situations are adequate for the communication system of the model nonhuman primate.

Each vocalization is discrete, representing a general situation in its totality. There is, however, a continuity of degrees of expression; the intonation, volume, register, duration, and amount of repetition of the vocalization represent the vocalizer's degree of involvement in the situation. Logically, the system as a whole is open, for new vocalizations taken as signs could conceivably be added to it. Practically, however, it is closed, for it is nonarbitrary; that is, the vocalizations are natural and thus a limited set of species-constant responses to various situations. Since only one vocalization is given for each general type of situation and responses are made to only a finite number of types (approximately twenty), there is also a finite number of possible combinations. Taken as signs, then, the number of situations that can be taken as signified, even in sequential combination, is finite. After a certain point, no new combinations could be made, so no new types or combinations of situations could be signified.

The vocalizations of the system are always responses to the direct presence either of the stimulus or a sign of the stimulus and are always taken as such. The nonhuman-primate sign system does not have the characteristic of displacement. Vocalizations cannot be taken as signs of objects that are not present to the vocalizer, nor can situations in the past or future be referred to. There is complete feedback of vocalizations; each individual hears the sounds he himself makes. He can and does, particularly in situations where he is startled, take his own vocalizations as signs.

Strictly speaking, nonhuman primates do not teach each other anything; teaching implies a conscious intention to impart information, and solid evidence of such an intention has not been observed in the behavior of nonhuman primates. They have great capacities for *learning*, as is demonstrated by their knowledge of and skill in utilizing various features of the physical environments they inhabit, but in the wild they learn their way of life without being *taught*. Scientists and circus trainers can teach them to do such things as eat with knives and forks and ride bicycles on tightropes by conditioning them with a system of rewards and punishments. In their native habitat, nonhuman primates learn what to expect from the physical environment through experience. At a very early age, infants and adolescents begin in play to imitate the behavior of their elders. Thus a major thing that young nonhuman primates learn is how to behave in the group. Social relations are extremely important among these group-living animals, and they begin to learn about them literally at their mother's breast. She exerts control over her child so that he learns that he is subordinate to those stronger than he. By the time he must fend for himself, he has observed how all the other members of the group behave. As an adolescent he observes all the ways of obtaining food—ways he must imitate if he is to survive. In his play he perfects such techniques as the proper way to mount females, or, in the case of females, to present oneself for mounting, or to establish and demonstrate dominance. Laboratory experiments involving the separation of infants from their mothers, and young individuals from the group, have shown that observation of adult behavior is essential to the development of skills necessary for survival. Individuals raised apart from the group do not learn proper techniques of foraging, for example, and may be so incompetent in copulation that they are incapable of reproducing. Thus, among the aspects of the physical environment that nonhuman primates take as signs, the most important is the behavior of their fellows.

Nonhuman primate group life leads directly to an endogamous sexual pattern. Since groups oppose one another, there is no breeding between individuals of separate groups; consequently, each group is inbred. Only very rarely does an individual, perhaps expelled from his own group, manage to join another group. However, the ways of life of geographically separated groups of nonhuman primates are very similar; this similarity can be taken as an argument both for the claim that their behavior is largely inherited and for the claim that their intellectual capacities restrict them to a relatively rigid pattern of responses to the physical environment. It is obvious that nonhuman primates (as well as men) do have inborn capacities for coping with problems and that the form—for example, shrieking and running for protection in the case of danger—if not the content—for example, shrieking in just this way and running slowly because the danger is distant—is determined within definable limits. Since all nonhuman primates are animals with similarly limited mental and physical capacities, we can expect that in relatively similar physical environments they will satisfy their basic requirements in similar ways. This is not to say vacuously that they behave the way they do because it is their nature to do so. It is rather to say that it is their nature to be capable of solving the basic problems of their existence in certain limited ways—that is, according to their limited level of intelligence—and that when these problems are set in a particular physical environment for different groups, the solutions devised by each group will be similar.

The fact that the use of physical objects as tools is practically unknown to them is evidence of the nonhuman primate's limited capacity for problem-solving. On rare occasions, nonhuman primates throw sticks or stones at an intruder. Very rarely, they actually modify some object for use as a tool, for example, stripping a grass stem for use in extracting termites from a nest. These examples of their use of tools appear insignificant when one considers how nonhuman primates could increase their food supply and their efficiency in collecting it simply by using a stick to dig up roots and knock down nuts and fruit. The same stick could be used to ward off marauders. In general, nonhuman primates do not use tools. They do not use tools for the same reason that they do not have a language; the limitations of their intelligence prevent them from advancing further in problem-solving.

In summary, nonhuman primates, according to this hypothetical model, must protect themselves, nourish themselves, and reproduce. The requirement for protection leads them to live in groups, and the imperatives of group life influence their behavior. They do not have language but take the behavior of their fellows as signs of environmental conditions. They are animals that are capable of solving the three basic problems of survival within the limits of their physical environment and their intelligence.

4 | THE PROTO-HUMAN

We now come to one of the most difficult and controversial issues in anthropology: Is it possible to postulate the existence of a proto-human animal, and if so, what is this animal like? We find it perfectly reasonable to think that in the course of man's evolution from his nonhuman primate ancestors there is a stage occupied by an animal that is no longer completely a nonhuman primate and yet not quite human. However, we need make no claims about the actual existence of the protohuman to find value in discussing what he would be like. The following synthesis is derived primarily from paleontological, archeological, and ethological data, but it relies less on data and more on logic than any of our other hypothetical models.

Anatomically, the protohuman differs from the nonhuman primate in several respects. His head is oriented the same way, but his brain is somewhat larger than the nonhuman primate's. More cortical area is devoted to the functions of the hands, thumbs, lips, and tongue, although not nearly to the extent that is common in man. The larynx and tongue of the protohuman are more efficient than the nonhuman primate's for the production of sounds through the motions of the respiratory and upper alimentary tracts.

The protohuman is an animal that stands and walks on two legs. To accommodate this posture, his pelvic girdle is shorter and broader and his spinal column more curved than the nonhuman primate's. The visceral organs are adjusted to an upright posture, whereas in the nonhuman primate they are oriented to a quadrupedal stance. The protohuman's arms are no longer than his legs, and they swing free as he walks. The opposability of the thumb to the four fingers of the hand is almost as precise as in man.

Sexual dimorphism is subdued in the protohuman. Males are somewhat larger than females, but the canine teeth of both sexes are about the same size and are not proportionately larger than their other teeth. Males weigh about 150 pounds; females, from 100 to 125 pounds. The maximum life span of both sexes is thirty-five years. Nubility is reached at the age of nine or ten, and full maturity at fourteen or fifteen. The length of life stages, as well as the complete life span are increased over those of nonhuman primates.

Females have periods of estrus throughout the year. They are sexually receptive much of the time and will present themselves for copulation even when they are not in estrus. Normally, only one infant is born at a time.

The protohuman is omnivorous. Protohumans eat more meat than do nonhuman primates, regularly capturing small animals for food.

Protohumans are adaptable to the same environmental ranges as nonhuman primates. They are anatomically less capable of protecting themselves from predators, however, because of the reduced size of their dentition and their correspondingly weaker jaws. They make up for this with increased intelligence.

Since protohumans are animals of the primate order, their solutions to the basic problems of life, determined by their requirements for protection, food, and reproduction, are structurally similar to those of the nonhuman primate. To secure protection, they live in groups. However, the internal organization of a protohuman group differs radically from that of a group of nonhuman primates because the unit is the nuclear family rather than the individual. Protohumans are born at an earlier stage of development than are nonhuman primates and are therefore more helpless and require a proportionately longer and more intensive period of maternal care. A nursing protohuman mother cannot be a completely efficient economic unit, so mating pairs stay together through the gestation period and while their offspring grow to maturity. Food collected is shared among the members of the family. Since a new child may be born before an adolescent separates himself entirely from his parents, mating pairs may stay together for many years to care for their successive offspring. The economic unit in the protohuman group, therefore, is a nuclear family: male, female, and one or more offspring. In situations where predators are not a danger, a family may be able to protect itself adequately, but in practice, protohuman families must join together in groups for the sake of protection.

Sexual behavior in a protohuman group varies considerably from that in a nonhuman primate group. As a rule, sexual relations are restricted to members of a mated pair. This pattern results from and reinforces the dominance pattern among the males. A male takes as his mate the female he desires most from among those not taken by more dominant males, and through dominance behavior he protects his right to her. He repels any sexual advances made to his mate by males outside his family as well as by adolescent males within it. Adolescent males are tolerated in the family until their maturing sexuality arouses the hostility of their male parent. Likewise, the adult female will tolerate her adolescent female offspring until they threaten her position; then she will drive them off. There are no functional restrictions to mating between male and female siblings in protohuman groups, and it is not uncommon. The economics of sharing food within a family also encourages monogamy. Polygamy, where a dominant male takes more than one mate at a time, is possible but impractical. It would be difficult for a single male to provide food for his family should he have more than one mate with a newborn infant at a time.

Since the economic unit of the protohuman group is the family, unmated males and females are not fully participating members of the group. They are less efficient at food gathering because family units, with the advantage of numbers, can push them aside, and they are not included in the reproduction plan. Because unmated males seek mates they are a menace to mated males, and so they may be expelled from the group. The group as a whole is hostile to other groups; therefore, each group is basically endogamous. However, since single males may be expelled regularly when there is a surplus of them in one group and since surplus females in other groups will be viewed with little sense of possessiveness by the mated males, exogamy is not uncommon. Males without mates in one group will take as mates surplus females from other groups. Whether the male remains with his mate's group or takes her to his own group probably depends on the degree of dominance he enjoys in each group. But if the female's attempts to remain with her own group overpower the male's attempts to take her away, the male will probably remain with her group.

The division of labor is determined by sex and age and follows particular family needs. When the female is burdened with a newborn infant, her mobility is restricted. The provision made for her by her mate may involve slight modifications of their customary food-gathering behavior. Since the male can range farther, he must carry food to his mate if he is to share it with her. Alternatively, he may call his mate to him when he finds food. Incidental sharing of food may occur whenever one individual happens to come upon another with food; however, the family structure provides a reason for sharing food regularly. Carrying and calling are logical consequences of the regular practice of sharing food. The protohuman's upright posture and ability to walk long distances make it possible for him to carry food home in his hands. The nonhuman primate, who is basically quadrupedal, cannot do this, and he must carry in his mouth anything he wishes to transport more than a few feet. The nonhuman primate does not, of course, carry or share food to any extent; what is significant here is that the bipedal gait frees the hands for carrying, which in turn frees the mouth for vocal communication.

Cooperation among individuals is required within the family. The benefits of such cooperation extend to the group as a whole through cooperation among families, particularly in hunting animals for food. Individuals in nonhuman primate groups sometimes hunt and capture animals, but they do not cooperate to hunt. Each individual is an economic unit, so food collecting is not a cooperative activity. Cooperative food gathering, including cooperative hunting, is a feature of the protohuman family that may readily be extended to the entire protohuman group. Cooperation among families for the purpose of hunting is probably more common than is non-antagonistic sharing of the kill. Perhaps the closest analogy to protohuman hunting behavior is that of carnivore packs, such as wolves. The prey is chased, surrounded, and overwhelmed. The sharing of the kill depends on the dominance pattern. When there is not enough for everyone, subordinate individuals get less or nothing. In such hunting packs males and females participate equally; this is also the case for protohuman hunters whenever females are not burdened by their young.

Cooperation and sharing within the family require some intentional communication on the part of its individual members. They can take place as occasional behavior, but to be economically effective they must be regularized by a system of communication. Cooperative and sharing behavior could be exhibited by individuals merely taking as signs the emotive cries of their fellows—running to one who has just vocalized as a response to his discovery of food, for example, in order to share this food. The protohuman improvement on the nonhuman primate system is that protohumans *intend* to call their fellows. A protohuman does not share food with members of his family simply because they either see or hear that he has discovered food and so come running to him. It is the purpose of his vocalization to call his family, and he sees to it that they understand and come. The meanings are taught and learned, and the communication system of the model protohuman is, therefore, a language. Unlike the nonhuman primate system, this system is two-way: there is intent to communicate on the part of the vocalizer as well as understanding on the part of the hearer that the vocalization is an intentional sign. The individual who has observed intentionality in his own behavior is able to interpret someone else's behavior as intentional.

The vocalizations of protohumans need not be different from those they would instinctively sound in various situations, nor need the number of different vocalizations that are intended as signs exceed the number that nonhuman primates take as signs. The difference between nonhuman and protohuman primate communication is one of intent. To mark this difference, we call any behavior or result of behavior intended for the purpose of communication a symbol. The possession of symbolic language makes the animals described in this chapter protohuman rather than nonhuman.

Cooperation and sharing can occur without language, but their value is vastly increased through the use of language. Hunting, as it is practiced by packs of wolves, for example, can reach highly effective stages, even though wolves have no language. They learn how to take the movements and vocalizations of their fellows and other animals as signs of behavior and of the state of the environment, but there is no evidence that one wolf intends to communicate to another the anticipation, frustration, and satisfaction that accompany the discovery, pursuit, and capture of prey. Wolves, like nonhuman primates, are intelligent enough to learn to take vocalizations as signs. They are not—as protohumans are—intelligent enough to intend their own vocalizations as signs. Therefore, they cannot plan or intentionally coordinate cooperative behavior; cooperation is largely instinctual when it occurs among them and is the result of conditioning when induced by human animal trainers.

It is worth examining two seeming exceptions to the claim that only protohumans and men have true language. Animals such as dogs and monkeys often behave in such a way that we say they are begging, either from men or from one another. But if we were to admit that they do beg, we would have to admit that they intend to communicate to another that they want something. This is almost certainly a false anthropomorphism. Their so-called begging behavior is instinctual. If such behavior results in satisfaction of desire, the animal will undoubtedly be conditioned to repeat it in similar situations.

The point at issue—intentionality—can be explicated even more clearly by an examination of the communication system of bees. When a bee has discovered food, he returns to the hive and goes through standardized motions before his fellow bees. These movements are determined by the distance and angle, with respect to the sun, of his flight back to the hive. Upon observing the motions, the other bees then fly off to the source of food. The behavior of the motioning bee is instinctive; it always follows the discovery of food. The behavior of his fellows after observing his movements is also instinctive; the character of his movements determines the direction and distance they fly for food. Unless we are completely wrong about the relation between brains and intelligence, not only is it most unlikely that a bee intends to communicate with his fellows, it would be a misrepresentation of the situation to say that the other bees take his movements as signs. It is likely that no bee understands or interprets anything as a sign. The food-gathering behavior of bees, like their protective and reproductive behavior, is instinctive. The behavior of nonhuman primates is, on the other hand, intelligent, and it involves a relatively large amount of understanding. But only among protohumans does communication behavior become intentional. What we wish to make clear here, without stating absolutely that chimpanzees, for example, do not intend to communicate with others, is that a highly effective system of communication, in which individuals take the vocalizations of others as signs, could *appear* to be intentional without necessarily being so.

The development of language is a logical outcome of the need for cooperative behavior. Alternatively, in a weaker sense, one can say that language use is the simplest logical step to take to improve the efficiency of cooperative behavior. Protohuman group life is a more advanced stage than the group life of nonhuman primates because of the improvements made possible by language. The protohuman's use of language to help solve the basic problems of animal existence is a manifestation of his intelligence. The rudimentary nature of his language reveals the limits of his intelligence. The development of language from a sign system, such as that described for the nonhuman primate, is an obvious step, but it cannot be taken without the intelligence.

Language use among protohumans, then, is basically related to cooperative behavior within the family and within the group of which individual families are the economic units. Let us now examine protohuman group structure in which there is elementary cooperation among families. In group behavior, cooperation is manifested first in the protection of the group. With intent understood, individuals are able to stand guard in order to watch for danger and to warn others of it. Even if there are no guards, each male watches over his family, but he does not warn them alone of danger. In defensive action, individuals can coordinate their activities; for example, some can hide while others run.

After its primary use in protection, the most valuable use of language by the group is in hunting. Some individuals can be positioned for an ambush, while others coordinate the movements of the hunt. Hunting as a regular activity requires several structural features in the group. There must be a core group of hunters, formed according to competence. Immature individuals and females with young are not capable of extended pursuit, and so are not included in the hunting group. They dig roots and gather vegetable food, saving some for the absent hunters. Thus, in contrast to nonhuman primate groups, protohuman groups do split up. Since the pursuit of ungulates may quickly take hunters some miles away from the rest of the group, and since the hunt is undertaken to secure food for the entire group, there must be a means for reuniting the group. This can be accomplished either by having one or more of the hunters return for those who stayed behind, or by establishing a meeting place to which the hunters return with the meat. Neither solution could be readily undertaken without language, unless the animals have instinctively established a home base, as wolves do with their dens, or are instinctively impelled to behave in such a way as to stimulate their fellows to go to the discovered food, as are bees.

It is not essential that a permanent home base be established, although this is the simplest solution to the problem of reuniting the group after separation, so a home base is usually established once the hunting territory has been defined. Individuals who become separated from the group can always find it again by returning to the home base. In addition, individuals who are injured, too sick, or too old to keep up with the group have more chance of surviving in a permanent home base, particularly if it offers some natural protection such as a rock shelter. Because food is carried to the home base and is shared with family members there, the sick and injured have some chance of recovery, and the elders a chance for longer life.

In contrast to nonhuman primates, who do not defend their whole range but only a central territory within it, protohumans must have exclusive access to a large territory, which they defend against other groups, if they are to be assured of a stable food supply. The defense of large territories enhances the possibilities of conflict between groups. If territories overlap, there will be conflict over the boundary. To avoid such undesirable encounters, protohuman group territories are usually separated by mutually accessible ranges. Nonhuman primate groups have as many as two hundred members, range over no more that fifteen square miles, and may reach a population density of more than ten per square mile. Protohuman groups, because of their hunting, may require as much as five to ten square miles per individual. Their groups seldom exceed sixty members, and the territory they defend may be as large as several hundred square miles. Remaining in such a territory is more efficient than migrating over a large range because the group learns in detail the physical characteristics of the territory and the habits of the animals that live there. It is apparent that the same physical environment is thus capable of supporting far *fewer* protohuman than nonhuman primates. The immediate reason for this is diet. Nonhuman primates eat vegetable food primarily, which is available in far greater quantity and variety than is the animal protein on which protohumans partially depend. In the ecological food pyramid, nonhuman primates are one step closer to the primary source of energy—solar radiation—because they are predominantly vegetarians. However, protohumans are partially dependent for food on animals that must in turn get their food from plants. The protohuman food base is more precarious to the extent that protohumans depend upon animal protein, which they must hunt, but it is more secure to the extent that they can eat both animals and vegetables. In terms of energy values, animal protein is far superior to vegetable, which means that the more successful the hunters are, the more easily assimilable and portable food of high nutritive value is available, which facilitates their further hunting success. The model protohuman and nonhuman primates are of similar size, and their diets are much the same except in the proportion of vegetable to animal food. But although the protohuman way of life includes distinctly improved methods of food procurement, fewer protohumans can be supported in a given area. The reasons for this decrease in total population despite improved methods of food procurement are basically cultural. If they were content with a vegetable diet, many more protohumans could be supported in an area of 200 to 300 square miles than the thirty to sixty who might defend that territory. But protohumans prefer to hunt for animal food, and the exigencies of social structure demanded by cooperative hunting as we have described it lead to sparser population densities than might be expected by an examination of the physical environment alone. It is primarily the *cultural* environment, not the physical, that determines protohuman population density.

The use of language to solve problems of existence in the physical environment gives rise to culture, which in turn influences protohuman behavior. Our presentation so far shows that the simplest use of language in the protohuman way of life is in the integration of cooperative behavior among the members of the group. We have in this process also described the simplest culture.

Protohuman primates also have definite traditions for the use and manufacture of tools, and in this they differ greatly from nonhuman primates. In a nonhuman primate group, the limited use and even the manufacture of tools could be passed on from generation to generation by way of observational learning. In such cases, tool activity, though it would be learned, would not be taught. No nonprimate tool-user or toolmaker intentionally passes on his skills, so he does not teach. Teaching is a form of intentional communication, combined with an intent to learn on the part of the learner. Intentional behavior is necessary to teaching, and teaching is essential for the transmission of cultural (as opposed to responsive) behavior from generation to generation.

Much of the protohuman's knowledge of social place and practices is gained through experience and observation, but there is some intentional instruction in the ways of social behavior among protohumans. Tool use and manufacture can be learned by observation. But to assure the permanence of tool traditions, they must be taught, and a tradition of their teaching must be taught. Nonhuman primates can learn to use tools, but such use is easily lost if the tool-users are inadequately observed and poorly or not at all imitated by members of the succeeding generation. The importance of language, and of teaching, to protohumans is that it does provide a cultural means for the transmission of knowledge from one generation to another. In protohuman groups such teaching is ritualized, the same tool-using and toolmaking techniques being passed on in the same way for generations.

If one asks as a logical question how tool use and manufacture might arise, there are many obvious ways, none of which can be logically shown to have preceded any of the others. Instances in nonhuman and protohuman life where very simple tool use would provide improved solutions to problems can be imagined easily. We have already discussed how improvement in nonhuman primate food-gathering techniques could be made by the use of a stick. Nonhuman primates do throw sticks that they have picked up off the ground, and even branches torn from trees. A logical step toward modification of a tool would be stripping down a branch, as chimpanzees have been observed doing with grass stems. The anatomy of primate arms makes throwing objects possible. What could be easier than picking up a stone and throwing it at an enemy? Stones might next be used in pounding or digging. Naturally sharp stones could be used in digging or cutting into roots or through tough animal skins. If no sharp stones are available, manufacture could begin from experience gained in pounding. Stones could be pounded against stones or bones to break off a sharp-edged tool. Tool use could also begin through the observation that rolling stones cause sparks and that sparks cause fires. Attempts to strike fires with two stones would be an example of tool use.

It is not our primary purpose to speculate on the actual origin of tool use and manufacture but to illustrate how it could begin. Primates are the only mammals that can stand and sit comfortably while at the same time having free use of their arms, hands, and feet for manipulating stones and other objects. However, the determining factor is neither the anatomical possibility nor the physical environment or situation that makes tool use appear to men so easy, so appropriate, and so logically fitting. It is the intelligence of the animal that determines whether a tool will be used, no matter how simple or complex its application may be. The associational and motor areas of the protohuman cortex are just adequate for recognizing and solving uncomplicated problems through the use of simple cutting, striking, and digging tools of stone, wood, and bone. This is not the case for the nonhuman primate, who is not able to recognize the nature of the problem.

Protohumans understand the use of fire. Their use of it is probably confined to heat for warmth and for cooking, light, and protection from animals. They have enough intelligence to pick it up, transport it, and replenish it, which nonhuman primates do not. Fires are most often hunted and taken into possession. This activity could have started, as hunting animals may have, through a form of scavenging. Once the value of fire is understood, fires started by lightning and volcanic eruptions are sought out. The difficulty in transporting fire is another factor leading to the establishment of a home base. It is probable that protohumans learn to make fire and that they regard this accomplishment as a very special skill. Fire making is almost certainly ritualized, and its makers may be regarded with awe. Speculation regarding the religious attitudes of protohumans is based almost completely on logic, but it is at least possible that fire rituals constitute the first and simplest religious celebrations.

Both cooperative hunting and tool manufacture involve planning for the future. Nonhuman primates seek out shelters that protect them for the night, but even their nest building is in response to immediate desires. If they seek a place of safety at dusk, it is because they are anxious for their safety then, not because they are preparing for the night ahead. Protohumans can plan ahead in hunting, in tool manufacture, and in the improvement of their home base shelters with brush or stone. To cooperate with others and to plan for the future, an individual must recognize himself as contrasted to others and as participating in the future. This kind of recognition is implicit in the cooperative family life of protohumans. Self-consciousness is coextensive with the intentionality of language use. The speaker recognizes himself as distinct from the individual with whom he intends to communicate. The first reflection of the grow-

ing concept of the self is the development of the concept of ownership. In a family situation, the male will think of his mate and offspring as his. In planning for the future, he will see future actions
and satisfactions as experiences that will belong to him. The food he
captures and carries is his, and it is shared with others. He will develop a sense of ownership of his tools, although tools are not logically necessary for the dawn of self-consciousness or the development of the notion of property. The group's territory and home
base are its property. One can see an analogy between such protohuman property and the nonhuman primate's dominance behavior
with respect to territory, food, and females in estrus. But the nonhuman primate does not have "property" because he has no consciousness of self. Consciousness of self and the notion of property,
early signs of the development of culture, arise only at that level of
intelligence which involves language use.

We have spoken so far of protohuman language as though it
consisted entirely of declaratives. In our characterization of protohuman language, we have said that the simplest coordination between meanings and vocalizations is not arbitrary; the protohuman
uses different, species-constant vocalizations as signs of what he
intends to communicate to his fellows. But it should be obvious
that if all he communicates is a description of his physical or emotional state or of the state of his surroundings, the cooperation and
planning we have described as parts of the protohuman way of life
would be impossible to integrate. A language composed merely of
declaratives would not lead to a way of life vastly improved over
that of the nonhuman primate, even if the declarations were intentional. Protohumans who plan and cooperate, besides being able to
express their physical and emotional states, must be able to give
commands and ask questions. Protohuman language must contain imperatives and interrogatives as well as declaratives. It is likely that
these forms are related to dominance behavior within the protohuman family. In his dominant position, the male organizes the activities of his mate and offspring. In their subordinate positions, the

female and the offspring will behave as the male desires. A dominant individual might convey a command by uttering a declarative while pushing his subordinate into the positions desired. A subordinate might ask a question by beginning the action thought to be desired by the dominant individual. An easier way to give commands and to ask questions would be to incorporate into language the recognition of self and others by adding sounds meaning "self" and "other," thus making possible imperative and interrogative moods. "Other" plus a declarative from a dominant to a subordinate would be a command, and "self" plus a declarative from a subordinate to a dominant would be a question.

Only the notions of commanding and questioning must be understandable to the protohuman. Once understood, they could just as well be conveyed by the intonation of a declarative, so that the same general vocalization with three different intonations could be intended and understood successively as declaration, command, and question. We speculate here about the possible logical relations between dominance behavior and imperatives and interrogatives in protohuman language. However tentative our conclusions about the origin and development of these language forms, it is without question that protohuman behavior as we have described it requires them.

Vocalizations in the language described so far make reference to total situations. If the notions of "self" and "other" are included in the language, a beginning is made toward the inclusion of names, which do not have reference to total situations but to individual things. Protohuman language must contain names of many common objects and places, such as tools and the home base.

But even this is not enough. Protohuman language must also contain ways of indicating the notions of affirmation and negation—notions embodied in traditional behavior, for example, in the recognition of permissible and forbidden forms of social interaction and in the standardizations of tool manufacture and fire use. And for planning it must have tenses so that the present can be distinguished from the future. In planning hunts protohumans must be able to talk of things that are removed from them in time and space. The co-operative behavior attributed to protohumans depends on language that enables an individual to express himself intentionally in the declarative, imperative, and interrogative moods, in the affirmative and negative, and in the past, present, and future tenses; and to use names that allow for reference to "self" and "other" and to common objects, places, and events.

We have concerned ourselves with the nonhuman and proto-human primates in order to be able to state explicitly those basic characteristics that are human. As can be anticipated, they are based primarily on the presence of symbolic behavior. The proto-human's symbolic behavior, expressed in his development and use of language, places him at a significantly higher level than the non-human primate. But his intelligence is still limited, and so, therefore, is his language. He does not have a sense of the pure arbitrariness of language, and each vocalization is a complete and fixed unit of expression. Not until we have an intelligence advanced enough to permit the development of a language of unlimited utility and productivity do we have an animal we can call human.

5 | ELEMENTAL MAN

Man does not differ radically from nonhuman and protohuman primates anatomically or physiologically; but he differs noticeably in his intelligence, which permits him to use a complex language of unlimited productivity and utility in solving the problems presented by the basic requirements of animal existence. For man, these requirements become conscious needs. Human language makes possible the myriad ways of manipulating other human beings and the physical environment, which are culturally expressed in hundreds of different forms of social institutions and material technologies. In constructing our model of man in this chapter, we shall discuss those features of human language and its use that show man to be a stage higher in intelligence than protohumans. The simplest and most logical social organization and technological development deriving from language use is presented in general terms as the way of life of elemental man. The rationale for the analysis of human language is primarily logical; for the analysis of culture, logical and anthropological.

The human body is the most complex physical system of its size in the known universe. The human brain is larger in absolute terms and in relation to body size than any other primate brain. It contains more neural cells and centrally associates more sensory stimuli and motor responses from a more complex synaptic nervous system than does any other primate brain. In man's brain the cerebral cortex is considerably larger in proportion to the rest of the brain than in other animals. The association areas and the sensory and motor areas for the hand, thumb, lips, and tongue are more than twice as extensive as in nonhuman primate and protohuman brains. A motor area found only in the human cortex, when stimulated, causes the human to vocalize continuously. In all these respects the human brain presents itself as the physiological foundation of human intelligence.

It is man's intelligent behavior that makes him distinctive; in appearance he closely resembles the protohuman. However, man stands straighter and strides more easily than the protohuman. His arms are shorter than his legs. Man is somewhat larger than the protohuman; he may reach 200 pounds in weight and as much as six feet in height, although females are generally slightly smaller than males. The opposability of man's thumb to the four fingers is greater than in the protohuman, and in the female the period of estrus is completely subdued. The cortical relations to these anatomical and physiological features appear in improved ways of getting and preparing food, in increased manual dexterity, and in mental control of sexual desire and behavior.

Because of evolutionary adjustments in the ilium for upright posture, the bony birth canal is narrower in man than in the protohuman. This means that the human fetus must be delivered earlier than is usual among other primates, at a stage when the head is still small enough to pass through the canal. As a result, the infant is particularly helpless and must be carried and cared for with constant attention for a number of months. Just as the period of infancy is longer among humans than among protohumans, so are the other life stages, and the life span for both sexes may exceed seventy years.

A distinctive feature of human babies is that their play antici-
pates their later intelligent behavior in two respects: (1) they
babble and (2) they manipulate every object they can lay their
hands on. The constant vocal play is soon channeled into learning
human language. Playing with objects finally results in facility in
the use of tools. Such play is an indication of a higher intelligence
than that of nonhuman primates, who neither babble nor play extensively with objects.

Individual men can exist alone, even when the physical environment contains many hazards, but man's particular ingenuity in solving the problems of securing protection, food and water, and a mate
seems best suited to group living. In addition, most men desire com-
panionship. Consequently, solitary individuals are as rare among
men as among the nonhuman and protohuman primates. The economic unit in the human group, as in the protohuman, is the family.
Polygyny and even polyandry are possible familial organizations, but
monogamy is most practical and remains the rule.

Unlike protohumans, men explicitly recognize kinship relations,
which are formalized in the ritual of marriage. Although the nuclear
family of two adults of opposite sex with their offspring is the basic
economic unit, the family can be extended to include the offspring's
mates and their children. Thus, the sense of kinship among men goes
well beyond the protohuman's sense of ownership of his immediate
family. Three to four generations may be represented within one
family group. The line of family classification may extend through
the father, the mother, or both. Males may bring their mates to the
enlarged families of their father, or females their mates to the enlarged families of their mother. These two arrangements are simplest, but the alignment need not be regularized, and various sorts of
arrangements may be made to keep the mated pair tied to both
parent families. It is important to understand that kinship relations
are socially recognized and can be, and often are, different from
actual biological relations. Frequently, in elemental human groups,
every individual is biologically related to every other in the group at

a removal of no more than three or four generations. Along kinship lines, however, the group might be strictly separated into several different patrilineal or matrilineal families. This discrepancy between the biological family and the kinship family is not uncommon among human groups.

Regulations based on kinship are cultural means of maintaining order. For example, incest is forbidden in all human families. The least extensive form of this prohibition forbids sexual relations between a parent and his or her immediate descendants and between brothers and sisters. Marriage between first cousins may be permitted, even preferred, although some human groups have elaborate codes that forbid sexual relations and marriage between the most remotely related kin. Kinship is a socially recognized relationship rather than a natural, or biological, relationship, and incest, which depends on kinship, is therefore a cultural prohibition.

Extended families include unmated adults and make possible their survival. Older adults whose mates have died still participate fully in the family and are cared for when they become feeble. Unmarried adult offspring also participate in the family, although their status is often inferior to that of their married brothers and sisters. Since children may be born at any time of the year and must be taken care of for so many years, individuals in human groups learn to interact constantly with persons of different age levels.

Division of labor is usually based rigidly on sex and age. This is in part biologically determined: the increased helplessness of newborn infants confines the mothers, who are restricted to some degree until their offspring reach adolescence; the increased length of time between infancy and adolescence means that there is a labor force able to take on simple tasks that are not too physically demanding. But it is also determined culturally: such activities as lengthy hunting trips away from the group are most effectively undertaken by adult males in their prime. Females, children, and old people generally gather vegetable foods and small game; they may, however, be employed as beaters to flush out game in mass hunts.

Cooperation of all sorts and the sharing of food are axiomatic in human groups. Sharing takes place according to several patterns based on kinship lines. Individuals learn by observation and instruction the socially expected ways of sharing and cooperating within the family. Such interaction is not restricted, however, to families, but extends to relations among families and among different human groups. Relations may be formalized according to kinship if the family is extended to the point where it is coextensive with one complete human group. Kinship lines may also extend among groups, formalizing sharing and cooperative behavior among them. This might occur when the offspring of two families in different groups marry. When marriage regulations are exogamous, which means that mates must be chosen outside one's own kinship line, and when this leads to the transfer of allegiance of one of the married pair from his former kinship affiliation to that of his new mate—which is not always the case—then there are situations in which different families and different groups provide mates for one another but are not related along kinship lines. Thus, families and groups have separate kinship lines but are biologically interrelated. The sharing and cooperation that often take place among these non–kin-related families and groups are mediated by the social institution of friendship. The simplest way to establish such friendship is through the mutual provision of mates to meet the requirements of exogamic marriage; exogamy reduces conflict within and between families and groups.

Family organization provides a logical source of leadership for extensive or complicated cooperative endeavors within and among families and groups. The head of a family has the greatest economic responsibility and the most experience in contending with the physical environment. The older he gets and the more experience he has had, the more authority he is likely to acquire. Dominance behavior in extended families is subdued: the family structure replaces the dominance pattern of nonhuman primate and protohuman groups as a means of securing internal cohesiveness. Between families within a group, dominance relations are not overt. Friendship and the value of cooperation between families in the group keep them together. If they disagree, they are as likely to separate as to fight. If a leader is needed for the cooperative activity of several families or several groups, the family head who best combines the virtues of age, experience, and friendly relations with others is the most likely to assume leadership without opposition. Several candidates who have ties of economics and friendship are as likely to share leadership as they are to fight over it.

It is apparent that even the simplest kinship pattern complicates the structure within and between elemental human groups far beyond that of protohuman groups. The advantage of social organization along kinship lines is that it formalizes and extends patterns of sharing and cooperation. It makes possible a more versatile and complex, and thus more efficient, attack on the problems stemming from basic human needs than is possible in other primate groups. The institution of kinship is, then, a major way of interacting with the physical environment and, hence, a *cultural* concept that makes the society of men distinctly different from that of protohuman and nonhuman primates.

The institution of kinship, as a way of organizing human groups for meeting their basic needs, depends on an elaborate language. Human language differs not in kind but in degree of logical complexity from that of the protohuman. The forms of this complexity are expressed in arbitrariness, productivity, and translatability, all of which facilitate man's consideration of objects and events displaced in space and time and make possible the transmission of knowledge by teaching.

The words, or vocalizations, in protohuman language refer to objects, actions, and expressions of facts, and are whole and complete in themselves. They are given either completely or not at all. In the simplest case these vocalizations are in part derivative from instinctive emotional cries and in part arbitrary. Such a language has a limited potential for expressing new ideas or combinations of ideas. Moreover, the all-or-nothing character of the vocal symbols means that the potential for translatability of the language—its capacity for repetition—is strictly determined: one individual can repeat only in exactly the same terms what another has said.

In human language, the basic vocal units are phonemes, discrete sounds having in themselves no semantic or reference value; these are combined into morphemes, which are words or parts of words that do have meaning. A very small number of phonemes, about forty in English, can be combined in an astronomical number of ways, which, even without repetitions, make possible a virtually unlimited production of different words. Since phonemes mean nothing in themselves, it is easy for us to recognize the arbitrariness of the words made from them. If human language did develop from instinctive emotive vocalizations, such roots cannot be traced now; in practice, all words in human language have arbitrary meanings. Any one morpheme is as capable of carrying any particular meaning as is any other, providing only that it is used consistently. This sense of the arbitrariness of language enables man to develop a language with a multitude of words expressing the same meaning, similar meanings, quite different meanings, and subtle shades of different meanings. The vast array of words, plus the ever-present possibility of making up new words arbitrarily to express new meanings, gives the language unlimited productivity: every human being can say many things during his lifetime that no one else has ever said before. The language also has translatability: unlike the protohuman, who is confined to repeating what he has heard in exactly the same terms as he heard it, man can repeat in other words what he has heard. The artistic creation of literature is the ultimate possibility afforded by these features of human language.

The discussion of things and events not present in space and time is made possible in human language generally by the use of tenseless names to refer to things and tensed verbs to refer to actions. By the form of the words used in discussion, one can indicate whether he is speaking of the past, the present, or the future. Language greatly facilitates discussion of things displaced in space and time, and it is therefore the most powerful method for transmitting traditional knowledge. Students can be told and can learn about what they have not experienced; teachers can convey knowledge of the past that no one will experience again, and provide advice for behavior in the future. One of the most distinctive features of human intelligence is the ability to recognize not only what is and what is not but also what might be and what might not be. The subjunctive form of speech is most important for expressing the possibilities of various plans of action. The ability to consider the truth of a counter-factual condition is at the heart of the human development of scientific knowledge. If it were impossible to say what the outcome might or might not be, or would or would not be, in the event an action does not take or has not taken place, then it would be impossible to explain the occurrence of particular events with reference to general laws. For example, you must be able to express in language your assurance that had we not written this book, you would not be reading it now, based on your confirmed belief that unwritten books cannot be read.

Humans differ from other primates in the ability to conceptualize. Human language as we have described it is an adjunct to the intellectual process of conceptualization. Human beings can generalize from their experience, expressing in thought, language, and action their conceptual understanding of themselves, their culture, and the physical environment. By forming concepts, man organizes his experience, classifying objects, actions, and events according to categories determined by degrees of similarity and difference. (Such conceptualization is expressed also—but on a much smaller scale—in the protohuman's conscious recognition of the self and others.) Conceptualization is an expression of the individual's ability to analyze relationships in such a way as to be able to see the general characteristics of a class manifested in a particular member of that class. He learns to expect from a particular the features and behavior common to its class, and he reacts to something new not with respect to its immediate particular characteristics, but with respect to the characteristics of the class to which it most appears to belong. Conceptualization, then, is a way of reacting to experience by organizing particulars according to ideal categories that have been derived from experience. It is a way of experiencing and coping with the world that allows a person to utilize his general knowledge in particular situations. Such classification is essential to all scientific knowledge—the general knowledge we can acquire from knowing what the characteristics are of this or that, what class it is a member of, what classes it is similar to and different from and in what specific ways.

In practice, conceptualization is a manifestation of man's ability to transfer to a new set of particular items the type of behavior characteristic of a previous similar set. Conceptualization is an expression of his ability to transfer the pattern of a solution of a problem from one set of circumstances to a similar set of circumstances. This is the intellectual essence of human behavior: in his interaction with the world, man forever generalizes from his experience, storing in his memory concepts of ideal types of things and, in particular, solutions to problems for use in future situations. Animals, which do not conceptualize, do in some cases manifest behavior that makes it appear that they do. Rats that learn a kind of maze in one box exhibit this problem-solving behavior when put in a similar box. However, the attribution of problem-solving conceptual powers to rats, for example, is erroneous anthropomorphism. Rats can be conditioned to behave (to solve problems) in certain ways in the presence of certain cues, but they do not understand (abstract and classify) the similarities of the problems or act according to a general plan. Even nonhuman primates acting in highly stylized ways in similar social situations are not manifesting self-conscious transference of standardized solutions of problems to other similar problems through conceptualization, but are responding in part through instinct and in part through conditioning to stimuli. Protohumans manifest a slight degree of self-consciousness. Intelligent problem-solving behavior is, however, the essence of self-conscious, human behavior.

Man's adeptness at solving problems, as manifested in his ready manipulation of abstract concepts, is first put to use in the exercise of tact and finesse in social relations, for example, in the institution of kinship. The fact that elemental man often has vast ranges or migrates is another indication of his ability to solve particular problems with reference to generalized solutions. His range is limited by extreme cold or heat, great expanses of ice or water, precipitous mountains and large deserts, and, most obviously, by the scarcity of food and water. Human groups may defend a territory, but they may also range so widely that they can defend only small parts of their territory at a time. They may have different territories at different seasons of the year, and rather than having a single home base, they may have several, each appropriate to particular stages of the hunt, or seasons of the wild-fruit or nut harvest. Moving into new areas, they solve many of the problems they face there with patterned solutions learned in similar situations elsewhere.

It is important to recognize how this migratory behavior of human groups differs from the behavior of nonhuman primates, which stay within a small range, and of migrating birds. The human's higher level of intelligence makes it easy for him to adjust to new environments. Nonhuman primates learn their way about a small range, but have difficulty transferring this knowledge to new ranges. Baboons, for example, generally react with fear when transplanted by man, and they seldom seek out new land on their own. As for migrating birds, a show of behavior alone is not adequate for demonstrating that problems are being solved with conceptualization. Behavior that is the result of instinct and conditioning in migrating birds is in man the result of intentional planning.

The use of conceptualized plans is found among protohumans in their standardized manufacture and use of tools—primarily, sticks for digging, thrusting, and throwing, and stones for pounding, chopping, and throwing. These types of tools are refined and varied by elemental man. To understand this variation, it is important to have a clear understanding of the concept of tools and the concepts of their manufacture and use.

Tools are physical objects purposively used to modify the physical environment. Language is also used to modify the environment, but it is not by this definition a tool. The world is full of physical objects that are immediately usable as tools, but these are not tools unless they are used by an animal to modify the physical environment for the purpose of satisfying his needs. We are tempted to say that only physical objects used with conscious intent to modify the physical environment are tools, if this were not too strict for traditional usage. Nonhuman primates use tools occasionally, but not with conscious intent, whereas protohumans and men use tools purposively and with conscious intent.

Primates use tools functionally in the same way they use their bodies. The entire body can be used as a projectile, and it can be used to pound and push. Arms and legs can be used for thrusting and prying, hands and feet for pushing and pulling. Fingers can be used for poking and prying, and fingernails and teeth for cutting. Elemental man uses tools as extensions of his body. The basic mechanical advantage he enjoys with tool use is the lever. The basic physical advantage he enjoys with tool use is sharper, harder, stronger, and better fitted, and therefore more effective, materials.

We have remarked that nonhuman primates could increase the effectiveness of their food procurement with nothing more than the use of a stick for digging and thrusting. They make practically no use of tools because they are not intelligent enough to understand the value of such behavior; this limitation is reflected by their inability to conceptualize and converse about tools, or anything else. The elemental human way of life includes the use of sticks and stones to push, pull, and cut in hundreds of standardized ways in hundreds of different situations. In each such situation a physical object, chosen for its suitable physical characteristics, is used as a tool, either in its natural state or modified. Logically, any sort of modification for use as a tool, even breaking a limb off a tree, constitutes manufacturing a tool. Both in choosing a natural object to be used as a tool and in manufacturing a tool, one must have knowledge of a desirable standard form. Nonhuman tool-users may appear to have such concepts, but only protohumans and men intentionally choose or manufacture tools with standard patterns in mind, and then proceed to use them according to a learned pattern. Nonhumans manufacture and use tools incidentally, as a result of instinct and conditioning.

Foresight—awareness of possibilities beyond the immediate situation—is required to do something secondary with intention (getting the tool by choosing an object or by modifying an object) to facilitate doing something primary (getting food). There is no logical difference between using a tool to modify another physical object to be used as food—as in pounding up grain with a stone—and using a tool to modify another physical object to be used as a tool—as in sharpening a cutting tool with a stone. The difference is entirely in purpose. A tool may be used directly to satisfy the needs for protection, nutrition, and reproduction, or it may be used to manufacture a tool to be used in turn for the direct satisfaction of these primary needs. For example, a sharp stone can be used to cut the flesh of an animal into pieces small enough to go into the mouth. Similarly, a stone can be used to pound another stone into pieces with sharp edges, which can be used as cutting tools. The kind of foresight required is not logically different in either case. In each case, the toolmaker has a result in mind that can be achieved through the use of a tool. But the degree of foresight required is different. Nonhuman primates do not use tools to make tools because they are not intelligent enough to see the more complex—although logically similar—problem. They rarely use natural objects as tools, modifying them with their hands or teeth, if at all; only protohumans and men use tools to make tools. The difference lies in relative intelligence. Such behavior is limited among protohumans by their weak conceptual powers; in man, the highest primate intelligence, a superior degree of foresight is manifested in the elaborate manufacture and use of tools. Man has at his disposal not only a large selection of tools, but also concepts of different types of tool use and manufacture, so that he is capable of innovating the manufacture and use of new tools in new situations. We have already alluded to the human power to invent new words, to form new abstract concepts, and to develop new forms of social organization. But the unique human capacity for creative thought and action is most strikingly expressed by innovative tool use and manufacture.

The elementary social organization and technology described in general terms above are used by groups of human beings as means of coping with the physical environment in a highly effective way. Man's conceptualizing intelligence, reflected in his use of language and tools, permits him to remember, solve problems, and plan over spans of many years. Man sees himself in time, which nonhuman and protohuman primates do not. Human cooperative activities, for protection from predators and weather, for hunting and gathering, and for procreation, can thus be organized and planned with conscious commitment of oneself and one's services for a week's hunt, a season's harvest, or a year's migration. Kinship commitments may be understood to extend over a lifetime. Certain forms of behavior, such as avoiding incest and building ties leading to peace and solidarity within and among families and groups, require more than intelligence. Self-control, which comes logically after the recognition of self, is essential to human group life. It depends on the individual's powers of foresight, that is, on his ability to recognize the value of behaving in ways that might be immediately unpleasant in order to attain long-range or eventual satisfaction of some need or desire. Foresight itself is just one manifestation of the ability to solve problems with the knowledge of what kinds of general results to expect in the event of various general circumstances. This application of conceptualization is usually called reasoning, and it is appropriate to say that the behavior we have described in this chapter is what leads to the designation of man as a rational animal.

Man's great ability to learn about his physical environment, about the habits of the animals he hunts and the growth patterns of the vegetable foods he collects, combined with his ability to use simple tools in a variety of ways enables elemental man to procure and use a great variety of foods. Many of these foods he modifies to make them more palatable by roasting, pounding, or soaking. He may store nuts and seeds for use when they are out of season, and preserve fruits and meat by drying them. He may use animal skins for warmth at night to supplement his hearth fire. But he is not master of the physical environment, nor does he command his food supply.

Elemental man is a very successful member of his ecological community, but he is not necessarily its dominant member. Despite his improved social and tool techniques, he usually does not disturb the ecological balance. Although he has improved techniques of food procurement, he may have less overall effect on the physical environment than the nonhuman primate because he develops tastes for only certain foods and does not exploit every possible food source. Man's social organization provides a cultural way of arranging separate groups so that each will have access to enough of the kinds of food it prefers. Since men desire meat, they must have large hunting territories. And since, in searching out only certain foods, they pass over many others that are edible, elemental men do not increase in population to the limits of the possible food supply but only to the limits of the preferred food supply. This is true for almost all other animals as well. However, the distinction is an important one to make for man because it is not until he learns to produce—not just to hunt and to gather in the wild—his preferred food supply, and to increase this production greatly, that human beings begin to increase greatly in population. Because of their specialized food interests, protohumans, elemental men, and advanced hunters and gatherers (who are treated in the next chapter) can be supported in successively smaller numbers in a given area than can nonhuman primates. Improved techniques in food procurement do not necessarily lead to greatly increased supplies of food and thus to an increased population. No particular social structure is necessarily related to the simple technology described above, but if language and tools together with a preference for meat do lead to cooperative hunting (which is a reasonable assumption), the result will be an extended range and a small population. An alternate *logical* possibility for elemental man is a high, concentrated population utilizing to its limit every possible food source. For cultural reasons, such a possibility is seldom actualized.

Economic success for the nonhuman primate is individual. Each nonhuman primate collects and consumes his own food. Among protohumans, the economic unit is the family. In the elemental human group it is clear that even the extended family is not necessarily the economic unit. The economic success of elemental man depends upon the cooperative activity of every individual and family within the group; the economic unit is thus the group, and the success of the elemental human way of life is group success. The amount of property owned by individuals and by groups is minimal; and, as a result, men on the elemental level get along better with one another, in families, and in groups than do any other primates, including men whose ways of life are outlined in the following chapters.

B | *Alteration of Nature*

6 | THE ADVANCED HUNTER AND GATHERER

6

THE ADVANCED HUNTER AND GATHERER

Man differs in physical and mental characteristics from the proto-human who in turn differs from the nonhuman primate, but all *men* —whatever their way of life—have, within very narrow limits, the same physical and mental structures. Racial differences in hair types, pigment, stature, and physiognomy are insignificant in comparison to the basic uniformity of brain size, construction of the hands, and motor abilities. In Chapters 3–5, the important distinctions are biological; in Chapters 6–10, they are entirely cultural.

The results of human cultural accomplishments are cumulative. Advanced hunters and gatherers, therefore, exhibit in most general terms the features of life of elemental man. The problem solved by elemental man with some degree of finality is the basic problem of individual and group survival. The way of life of elemental man, with its social stress on cooperation and sharing, provides the best possible way for assuring the protection of the individual within the group and of the group itself. This is the human way, and it is basic to human life at every stage. On the elemental level, it becomes highly unlikely that a human group will be overwhelmed by preda-tors if the group has time to set up its defense or that it will be destroyed by adverse effects of climate if there is a place to which it can migrate. We can assume that advanced hunters and gatherers employ these methods of protection. They differ from elemental man in their development of more complex tools and techniques for procuring food, but these do have limitations: first, the primary methods of obtaining food are still hunting and gathering, and second, the tools used are entirely man-powered.

Advanced hunters and gatherers improve the quality and stabilize the quantity of their food supplies through two specializations: herd hunting of one or several species of large animals, rather than pursuing individual animals, and intensified collecting of one or several of the more abundant wild grains, seeds, nuts, fruits, and roots, rather than random gathering. This way of life brings man into close association with the animals and plants he lives on. He must learn the behavior patterns of the animals; he must know when they group together, when the young are born, and the courses of their daily movements or seasonal migrations. Similarly, he must know the habitats in which plants grow and the seasons in which their fruits can be harvested. The way of life of the advanced hunter and gatherer is at least seasonally sedentary. Herds do not travel incessantly; plants do not bear fruit all at once, nor can they be harvested in a day. As animals and plants are followed throughout their seasonal cycles, the men who live off them establish seasonal home bases. These temporary camps also provide the necessary storage and redistribution points for food collected by individual members, which will be shared by the entire group. If food procurement is sharply curtailed at some seasons because of weather or fruiting cycles, it may be convenient to establish one central home base where food supplies can be stored all year and perhaps protected by some permanent residents.

The tools of advanced hunters and gatherers are more specialized and more complex than those of elemental man. Elemental man uses no compound tools, whereas they are characteristic of advanced hunting and gathering. The simplest compound tool is a spear, fashioned from a stick and a pointed stone or piece of bone. This is a combination of a wooden spear (which elemental man pointed by carving or by burning the end to a point in a fire) and the hard point and cutting edge of stone or bone. A more complex type of spear is made with a removable barbed spear point set in the end of a wooden spear and attached to it by a length of cord; the spear itself is thrown with a spear thrower. The barbed point is difficult to pull out; the spear shaft dangling on the cord makes it difficult for the animal to run; and the increase in arm length provided by the spear thrower makes a harder and longer throw possible. This weapon is a great technological improvement over the wooden spear.

The manufacture of compound tools depends largely on the technique of hafting (supplying a handle). Stone and bone tools equipped with handles are easier to use, and the handles, especially on mauls and axes, make efficient levers.

The cutting possibilities of worked stones are also enhanced by hafting. With the addition of handles or shafts, small blades and microliths become usable in place of the large, brittle blades that are in themselves tools; set into shafts, which provide the flexible strength of wooden backings, they make a variety of tools depending on the type of hafting: knife or sickle, arrow, barbed spear or harpoon, scraper, and awl or drill. Development of such tools as sickles, which are used in harvesting wild-grass seeds, involves two steps. Man must first recognize the value of combining the two materials, wood or bone and stone, to make a tool. This leads to the manufacture of small blades and microliths, for example, which may not be easily usable as tools in their own right, and wooden or bone handles, which have little use until they are set with blades. We can make a cautious analogy here with human language, which has meaningless phonemes that can be combined into meaningful morphemes. The analogy is not exact, but the parts of a compound tool are certainly of less use (if any) as tools in themselves than is the complex finished tool compounded from them. The potential for variety is greatly increased by compounding elements. The ability to join pieces together into compound units in this fashion is a measure of human intelligence. Once man recognizes the possibility of making an improved tool by putting pieces together, he must solve the problem of fastening them together. This is accomplished in one or a combination of three basic ways: wedging, tying or wrapping with skin or cord, and gluing with adhesives such as pine resin and asphalt.

Tools constructed for specific tasks are more effective, often because they combine the best aspects of two simple tools. A hunter can try to stop a running animal by throwing a stone or by entangling the animal in a cord. But if he ties stones onto lengths of cord and then ties the loose ends of the cords together, the composite weapon thus constructed is much surer and more efficient than is any one of its parts used alone.

In the development of weapons, greater force and accuracy is gained by redirecting and channeling forces. The flight of a spear, for example, is improved by the use of a symmetrical point and a smooth, straight shaft. If such a weapon is thrown with the hand alone or with a spear thrower, it must be relatively heavy for a man to be able to throw it any distance with force and accuracy. The spear can be lightened and shortened to make an arrow, which, though it cannot be thrown by a man with any force and accuracy for any great distance, can be shot with a bow a much greater distance with more force and accuracy than any spear can be thrown. The bow redirects muscle energy, channeling it along a confined course. In the case of the bow and arrow, this happens when a man exerts one set of forces— the push against the bow and the pull on its string—concentrating these forces in the tensed bow. When the string is released, these forces are redirected along the narrow flight line of the arrow. This channeling of force is also a principle of the blowpipe. A man can exert very little force simply by blowing. But when the arrow is reduced to the size of a dart and is inserted in a long, smooth tube, the force of a man blowing into the tube is sufficient to propel a light dart great distances with force and accuracy.

There are then, three levels of tool complexity: (1) simple tools, such as pounding and cutting stones; (2) compound tools, such as the spear and axe, powered directly by human force; and (3) tools such as the bow and blowpipe, which redirect and channel human energy for more efficient use of another tool. These three levels of tool complexity correspond to three levels of efficiency in the use of energy. The man who pounds with a stone has far less efficiency than the man who is able to give his energy greater direction through the use of hafted tools. On the third level, that of redirected energy, man is able to channel the full force of his body into specific and sometimes minute tasks. The use of a bow drill, for example, channels much greater energy onto a specific small point than a man can impose either by using a simple implement held in the hand or by hitting a punch with a hafted maul.

The manufacture of compound tools certainly grows out of the manufacture of simple tools. To put two tools together, man must obviously make one of them first. This is a matter of the simplest logic. And as a matter of logic we describe an elemental human way of life that includes the manufacture of only simple tools in contrast with the way of life of the advanced hunter and gatherer in which compound tools are manufactured and used. These syntheses depend to a large extent on archeological and ethnographical data as well as logic. Nevertheless, it is not necessary to postulate that any given group that has compound tools must pass through a way of life that involves simple tools alone. Once the notion of tool use and manufacture is understood, simple and compound tools can easily be developed at the same time in the same group.

That the earth's materials can be used as building blocks is apparent to elemental man. He puts up walls of stone and constructs rude shelters of branches. The compound tools of advanced hunters and gatherers are the result of extending this basic notion of constructive organization. Man can do more than pick up material objects to use as tools and improve these materials in certain ways; he can also combine these materials in various ways.

The most important way of holding things together is tying—the basic principle of weaving and sewing. Branches can be threaded together, but they can be held most securely by being tied with a flexible vine or with a cord made from a strip of skin. This is the simplest way to improve a shelter. The value of covering a framework of branches with skins as protection from the weather is obvious; skins tied together afford even greater protection. Skins worn as clothes must also be tied on in some way. A punch can be used to make the holes in the skins necessary to tie them together. The use of needle and thread is an improved specialization on cruder techniques of lacing and tying skins together. Plaiting and weaving are improvements on a technique employed most crudely on flexible branches and more easily with strips of skin. Such compounding is important in making shelters and clothes as protection from the weather, but is also extremely important in making containers for carrying and storing food.

The techniques of building frameworks of branches and of sewing skins together are combined in making tents, which greatly extend man's range. With a tent man can survive colder nights than he can in the open, and in a tent he can protect himself from the rigors of bad weather. A portable tent provides a more adaptable home base than would most of the natural shelters or permanent structures that a hunter and gatherer might find or be able to build where he wants to stay. In shelter, clothes, and containers, the flexible sewn materials make man's way of life itself more flexible.

With a shift in the design of sewn skin over a framework of branches, man can construct a boat instead of a tent. Like the tent, the boat also greatly extends man's range. Elemental man crossed rivers on floating logs, and he even hollowed out logs to make boats. But skin boats are portable and more maneuverable. They extend man's range onto large bodies of water, making it possible for him to hunt marine animals and to fish (a form of hunting). The specialized and complicated gear of arctic hunters shows how capable man is of conceiving and manufacturing compound tools to protect himself and to procure food in the harshest of environments.

With such control over materials, advanced hunters and gatherers are able to exert an important influence on the physical environment. The ways of life of the nonhuman primate, the protohuman, and elemental man are in large part controlled by the physical environment. These groups live primarily in ecologic balance with the natural environment, affecting it in ways and to degrees no different from other large animals. Even elemental man is by no means always the dominant member of his ecological community. The balances of energy exchange in a community of which elemental man is a part might be very similar to those in a community in which some large ungulate, rather than man, is the primary member. The physical environment sets the problems for nonhumans, protohumans, and elemental men; their solutions to these problems do not disrupt the basic balance of the system, and their numbers are rigidly controlled by the food supply, which is determined by forces over which they have little if any control. Advanced hunters and gatherers do not have direct control of their natural environment, but they do have a great effect on it. They are always the dominant animals in the ecological communities of which they are a part, and the balance of animal energy exchange in the community is best understood by taking them as the basic influence.

Advanced hunters and gatherers are the major predators in the communities they inhabit. They are successful to a degree that pushes out other large predators, and they also eliminate competition by hunting these predators themselves. The hunting pattern of the advanced hunters and gatherers is more efficient than that of elemental man. Elemental man hunts individual animals, perhaps pursuing them for days over long distances. Many advanced hunters and gatherers, on the contrary, establish relations with a specific herd (or herds) of animals, taking their prey selectively from the herd. They adjust their way of life to the way of the herd they are following. If the herd migrates from one area to another following seasonal grazing, so does the group of men that hunts it. This places a premium on the lightness and portability of goods, and on the development of shelters and social institutions appropriate to a nomadic way of life. In such a situation the skin, bone, and other products from the animal hunted are among the most frequently available materials, so many tools are made from them. While the development of intricate and compound tools for specialized purposes leads to definite orders of private ownership, from a pride of craftsmanship and possession as well as from usefulness, such possessions are few because of the need to travel. On the other hand, the notions of territory as a group possession are expanded to include definite feelings of group ownership of the herds being followed. Besides proprietorship, some concern for conservation may enter: hunters may take primarily old and young animals and leave those of breeding age to sustain the herd. Herd hunting tends to consolidate the human group, keeping it together with the herd. It regularizes the procurement and supply of food, and because fewer hunters are needed to supply food for the group, it often leads to a certain division of labor among the men: the more adept hunters will do more of the hunting than the others. When fewer men do the actual hunting but all must share the kill, the formalization of sharing is intensified. As among groups of elemental men, the lines of distribution follow those of kinship.

Advanced hunters and gatherers, adept at utilizing many natural materials in the production of tools and very efficient as hunters and gatherers, dominate the animal community, and should they be removed from it (as has happened recently in Africa where contemporary hunters and gatherers have been excluded from areas designated as animal preserves), radical adjustments sometimes occur in both animal and plant distributions as a new balance without man is established. Since man, as an advanced hunter and gatherer, is the major predator, his activities do determine to a large degree the species and numbers of animals in the community and also, to some extent, those of plants. This is the first way of life among those described so far in which man has a definite altering effect on the environment. Advanced hunters and gatherers are certainly aware of their effect; such awareness, with the suggestion it gives of even greater influence, if not control, provides the intellectual stimulus for the development of advanced hunting and gathering technologies, so many of which are intricately adapted to the efficient exploitation of various environments.

Advanced gathering techniques, which reflect man's ability to collect wild-grass seeds in abundance, for example, probably lead to the later notion of cultivating grains. Scythes and flails, as well as shovels and hafted digging sticks, greatly enhance the ability of women, children, and old people to add to the food supply. Equally important are skin bags and plaited baskets, in which seeds and roots can be gathered and carried.

Herd hunting thus assures the food supply, but so do the improved tools and techniques for gathering. Associated with both of these are improved methods of preparing food. Tools such as the fire drill make the employment of fire common for advanced hunters and gatherers, so roasting and baking game are ordinary methods of cooking. Containers make it possible to collect and save large quantities of wild seeds, which can be ground into meal. Containers also make it possible to boil foods in water that is heated by dropping hot stones into it. Tough foods are improved simply by pounding or by soaking them in containers of water. Such methods of food preparation make it possible to utilize a large variety of foods; however, they can lead to the concentration on specific types once easy ways of using them are found. Herd hunters certainly concentrate on one or a few types of animals, and if they continually move about on grasslands following ungulate herds, they may also concentrate on the collection of wild-grass seeds.

Since the problems of protection are not paramount for advanced hunters and gatherers, and since their techniques for procuring food are highly efficient, it might seem that they would reproduce in large numbers. On the contrary, because of the highly specialized diet, it takes a larger territory to support a group of advanced hunters and gatherers than it does to support the same number of elemental men, just as the relative specialization of the diet of elemental man means that a given area can support fewer men living the elemental human way of life than protohumans or nonhuman primates. The improved technology makes possible the utilization and preparation of more foods at a higher quality level; specialization of the diet means that there is really less food than there would be with a simpler technology. The population of advanced hunter and gatherer groups is not determined by the absolute food supply but by a cultural preference for a part of it. In some extreme environments, however, such as the Arctic, where every food possibility must be exploited if men are to survive at all, the potentiality of advanced hunting and gathering technologies for procuring all possible food is actually developed. This demonstrates that almost all food sources can be exploited when necessary, although usually they are not.

The food specialization of advanced hunters and gatherers leads to warfare among groups who live this way of life. Man is the only animal that murders, since murder involves killing with conscious intent. Other animals sometimes kill members of their own species, and some groups of ants, for example, battle with other groups of ants. Only among men, however, can intentional plans for killing—whether of prey or of one's own kind—be devised Among groups of advanced hunters and gatherers, the killing of one's own kind from other groups is formalized in the institution of warfare. Leadership in war, like that in hunting and in other affairs, devolves on the most experienced and adept. In ordinary circumstances, such warfare is an aspect of protection. The group must defend the territory on which it hunts, and particularly the herds it follows. If another group of men contests their ownership, the two groups may resort to battle to settle the issue. The elemental way of life makes it easier for groups to move apart than to battle. But because of food specialization it may not be possible for a group to move to another area and support itself. Conflict is usually lessened by relations of kinship and friendship based on exogamic marriage. But if two groups are too large to be supported on one territory, then it becomes a matter of life and death to possess a territory and the herds on it, and warfare between the two groups may follow.

Warfare, like herd hunting with its necessity for cooperation, intensifies the need for group cohesion. To this end the customs of group behavior will be made more explicit in the form of rules or norms of conduct. The basis of the normative system is in family relationships, and the normative structure follows that of kinship cooperation and sharing. Punishment by the group or by leaders representing the group will be meted out to transgressors of norms. For almost all deviant behavior, group ostracism of some sort is sufficient to bring the offender back into line. But anyone who breaks a rule dictating behavior that the group considers essential to its survival may be banished or even killed. What might appear to be an unfair expression of this principle occurs in the exposure of infants—most often female—if their care and feeding would impose hardship on the group. Such killing of infants benefits the parents as members of the group, since the infant individuals endanger the group's survival by putting unfulfillable demands on the food base. Thus, all three sorts of killing of human beings by the group appear *murder* to derive from the same principle, group protection: individuals of other groups willfully trespassing on the defending group's territory may have to be killed to protect the territory, which is the food base; individuals within the group who seriously transgress norms essential to group cohesion may have to be killed to reestablish harmony; and infants who cannot be raised on the group's food base may have to be killed to keep the group's size in balance with its food supply.

A fourth reason for killing men is to augment the food supply. Individuals of other groups can be hunted just as can other large animals. Cannibalism, however, usually arises only in cases of extreme need because of the social ties relating groups and individuals and also because men are very dangerous prey. It is more often practiced ritually, for purposes of group cohesion.

An important way of assuring group cohesion is the ritual initiation into the body of mature individuals in the group. In an initiation ceremony, individuals who have just reached adulthood may be impressed with the gravity of the normative rules of the society and may be made members of an organization that goes beyond kinship lines and exists primarily for the purposes of increasing loyalty to the group. Such initiation ceremonies have an obvious economic function. Human beings reach sexual maturity before they attain complete intellectual and bodily growth. By delaying initiation into adulthood until an individual is intellectually and physically, as well as sexually, mature, the group protects itself by making sure that its members are not allowed to marry and produce children until they are capable of providing for themselves and their offspring.

Initiation rituals may lead to cosmological and religious speculation. In providing explanations for the rituals and for the genesis and importance of the norms of the group, some attempt may be made to understand man's place in the physical environment and the significance of his possession of self-consciousness. These ceremonies might be conducted by specially talented individuals with a flair for emotionalism and showmanship, who might be considered analogous to members of the priest classes of more complex ways of life, although their skills need not necessarily set them off as more important to the group than, for example, a particularly skilled maker of arrows.

In speculating about himself and his place in the cosmos, man will certainly face the fact of death. He kills animals for food and other men for his own protection. He is the only animal intelligent enough to realize that he too must die. Since he also sees himself in time, as having had past and expecting future experiences, he will be led to wonder what happens to him after his death. If he believes that the power of animals resides in their bodies, he may eat some part of the enemies he has killed, or of his parents when they die, in ritualized cannibalism to gain their strength. If he believes that the spirit of a man lives on after death, in this world or another, he may bury the bodies of his dead out of fear or respect and bury with them valuable artifacts to keep them from bothering the living, or to serve them in the other world.

We are justified in postulating on technological grounds the presence of painting and sculpture among the cultural developments of the advanced hunter and gatherer. Advanced hunters and gatherers extensively utilize constructive methods: they put together various materials to make such things as shelters, clothes, and boats. They make tools by combining elements that in themselves are not usable—or at least not very efficient—as tools. They see how the basic properties of materials can be combined to make compound and complex tools that are such improvements over simple tools that they appear not as mere modifications of natural objects but as new creations. To mold clay or carve bone into the form of an animal or to spread pigment on a wall in the outline of a man is an even further possible extension of materials. Artistic constructions are quite removed as objects from the materials out of which they are constructed. What must be understood technologically is what characteristics of various materials can be used to achieve the desired results. If one considers artistic forms in relation to language, as symbols, they are logically equivalent to spoken words. They are more than pieces of clay or pigments; they have meaning given to them by man. It is surely reasonable to suppose that craftsmen who are skilled in the production of complex tools are capable of conceiving and executing the construction of such complex art forms as sculpture and painting.

In Chapter 5 man was introduced as an animal that attacks with conscious intent the problems arising from his basic needs. Man adds purposiveness—his own—to the ecological system of which he is a part. In the elemental way of life he is controlled by the physical environment as much as any other animal. As an advanced hunter and gatherer, he preys on selected animals and plants for food in the environment and is so successful that he alters the ecological balance. He pursues his satisfactions intentionally, and even controls animal populations through selective herd hunting, but the ecological effect he has on the environment is not intentional. He may cause great changes, for example, when he hunts by setting brush or grass fires, but his intention is the capture of certain animals, not the alteration of ecological succession among plants, and thus among animals. Nevertheless, advanced hunters and gatherers exert a conscious control over materials with their skilled manufacture of complex tools. And they are aware of the effects they have on plant and animal populations as a result of their hunting and gathering, even if the imperatives of their way of life do not allow them to manipulate their activities in such a way as to control these effects extensively.

Elemental man does not have enough effect on the physical environment to give him the notion that he might control nature rather than be controlled by it. His way of life involves the use of tools, but he could survive without them. The advanced hunter and gatherer sees and actualizes to a slight degree the possibility of controlling nature, and he does alter it. His way of life depends on the use of tools.

C Control of Nature

pop. increase because
less terr. is needed
to support

7

THE DOMESTICATOR OF PLANTS AND ANIMALS

Advanced hunters and gatherers are nomadic to the extent required by the animals they hunt and the plants they collect, but they are semi-sedentary according to the seasonal life cycles of these animals and plants. And, in those times when men are living on stored food, they may have regularly recurring blocks of leisure time for craft specialization, art, and speculation. Semi-sedentary conditions are essential also to the development of the invention that has had the most revolutionary impact on man's way of life: domestication of plants and animals. Elemental men are simply important animals in the ecological community; advanced hunters and gatherers have an important effect on the ecological community, but do not control it; domesticators of plants and animals, however, exert a great deal of influence on the physical environment and often actually control its ecological balance. Domestication has revolutionary importance because it results in a kind of food specialization that makes possible a vast increase in the quantity and degree of stabilization of the food supply. This potentially great increase in food supplies, if realized, allows for a resultant, correlative increase in population, and since large populations are necessary for the development of the civilized way of life, domestication is at the foundation of civilization.

Let us begin with the essential territorial requirements for the domesticators' way of life. The physical environment must contain plants and animals amenable to domestication. Among animals, those that live in herds are most easily domesticated. Herd behavior is such that most animals follow the lead of some dominant member or all members stay close together and move together. If a man can gain control of the movements of a few members of a herd, the other members will be likely to follow. Among plants, those like the grasses, which tend to grow densely and widely at the expense of other species, and tropical plants, which are easily transplanted, are most amenable to control by man, although it is highly unlikely that these plants, or any others, would be domesticated at any great distance from places where they grow naturally.

Domesticators must also have a semi-sedentary way of life. People who are continually on the move do not have time to experiment with domestication, but people who have at least seasonal home bases will probably observe two things that suggest the possibility of domestication. Around the areas where wild grain and seeds are stored or eaten or where garbage is thrown, plants grow from lost seeds. Men are certain to take advantage of these accidentally sown plants, harvesting them even though they were not intentionally planted. Young animals that have been captured alive by hunters will probably be brought to the home base. Such animals are dependent on the people who tether or cage them, and often become quite tame. They are obviously a potential food source, even though they were not consciously captured for this purpose.

A semi-sedentary life in a physical environment with appropriately domesticable species is a necessary but not sufficient condition for the invention of domestication. Man must also be, and is, intelligent enough to understand the possibilities and to act on them. What a semi-sedentary way of life provides, with regularly recurring intervals of leisure, is the time and place for experimentation.

We still cannot say that in such conditions domestication is necessarily invented; however, these are the conditions under which it could and most likely would be invented by man.

Men who live a way of life in which they are primarily dependent on domesticated plants and animals for food are more bound to limited areas than are elemental men or advanced hunters and gatherers. The latter feel a sense of ownership of the wild plants and animals on their territory, but their degree of control over these plants and animals is small. Domesticators, who have direct control over domesticated plants and animals, have an explicit notion of property; they can manipulate and dispose of property as they will. And since it is necessary for the growth of their domesticates that sufficient land be available, the notion of territory that belongs to the group is refined: land becomes property that is more consciously and explicitly owned, either privately or communally, than is the territory of elemental men or of advanced hunters and gatherers. To the extent that the entire group still depends on the joint produce of its members, property will be communal. However, work and distribution along kinship lines—which is most likely—tends to divide communal property into family holdings. The very great productivity of farming and herding is what permits this separation. Each family can, through its own labor, produce enough food for its own needs. In the simplest situation, work can be organized and supervised along kinship lines, with each family maintaining its own flocks and fields. Each family would ordinarily be self-sufficient, but in times of need could share the produce of other families in the group.

Farmers who concentrate mostly on the growing of plants have territories—or land holdings—which are extremely small compared to those of hunters and gatherers. An extended family of a dozen members may farm no more than a few acres. A dozen such families grouped together in a village community may hold no more than a few square miles of land, the bulk of which would be grazing land for the herds or flocks. Herdsmen, who concentrate mostly on the nurture of their animals, usually have much larger territorial claims than farmers. Larger herds and flocks will require more grazing land and not uncommonly will force the herdsmen to migrate seasonally for hundreds of miles with their animals to find adequate supplies of grass. Even such nomads, however, may own fields in which they sow grain at one season, returning to reap their crop at a later season. Agriculture and animal husbandry are usually combined to some degree, although absolute specialization in one or the other is a possible self-sufficient way of life.

Small village communities offer many advantages to predominantly agricultural people. Several families can group their houses, storage bins, and stables together in order to provide protection for themselves, their stored foods, and their animals. A substantial body of people is also available in case of need to defend growing crops or flocks in the field. No special group organization beyond that of the advanced hunters and gatherers is necessary for a small village community. However, the amount of property owned by individuals and families gives rise to problems of ownership. Most basic are those concerning ownership of house and field plots. Property lines are established through mutual agreement and by occupation of worked plots of land, with disputes mediated by the more experienced and respected members of the village community. These community leaders are also most likely to take charge of communal distribution of food supplies in case of group shortages due to crop failure, raiding, or other reasons.

A crisis might arise in a village community from population increase as a result of substantial food production. If an extended family grows too large to be supported on its land holdings, then new holdings will have to be found. If open land is not available within a reasonable distance from the village, men may set out to establish villages of their own on new territory. Such expansion will first occur throughout areas where agriculture is supported by natural precipitation. However, if fields are irrigated, crops can be grown in drier climates than would support the plants normally.

Once agriculture is established in temperate lands, the need for the proper amount of rain to fall on the crops at the proper time is established as one of man's enduring topics of conversation. The relationship between growing plants and water is easily enough understood, and where rainfall is insufficient most men are probably intelligent enough to see the possibility of carrying water from rivers or springs to the fields or of digging artificial channels to divert water from these sources to the fields. We cannot say what it takes to motivate men to actualize such possibilities, but need in time of drought would surely be enough in some cases. When village farmers do move out of the areas in which their crops will ordinarily grow under natural rainfall to areas so dry that irrigation is necessary, then they begin to exert even greater control over the environment than before and thus become dependent on an artificial environment they create. Agriculture might also begin in marginal areas where rivers provide naturally irrigated flood plains.

The development of agriculture and animal husbandry in itself suggests a climate of thought in which men are receptive to innovation; that is, the domestication of plants and animals requires some experimentation. Men must choose and try various species; they must think of possibilities, plan in order to actualize these possibilities, and then evaluate the results. Even if domestication arose out of accidental garbage-plot gardens and keeping pets, once it suggested a way of life, men would experiment with different species and ways of growing them, sometimes through the force of circumstances but also out of curiosity. Besides direct concerns with animals and plants, efforts would be expended on the invention and elaboration of tools to care for them. Although all individuals of a given age and sex would be engaged in more or less the same kinds of work for subsistence, they would naturally tend to specialize in different crafts. A partial division of labor could thus develop. There would also be individual specialization in the conduct of ritualistic celebrations and in the production of art forms. Craft, ritual, and art skills might be perfected further in games and contests of some utilitarian value.

The domesticator's way of life is adaptable to many different environments. Just as the overall pattern of the way of life of hunters and gatherers might be followed in various plant and animal environments, so might the techniques of domestication, agriculture, and animal husbandry. In many cases, it is the pattern alone that is transferred from one environment and one group of people to another, rather than the content. However, many domesticated plants and animals are also quite adaptable to new environments, and so are transferred along with the way of life. Domesticators improve their crops and animals by breeding selectively for large, healthy, and manageable producers. It is both the wide applicability of the pattern and the malleability of the domesticates that permit the wide distribution of this way of life.

To be potential domesticates, plants and animals must occur in sufficient numbers and be hardy enough to survive the changes man imposes on them by confining them to ways that suit his own purposes. They must be able not only to survive but to respond to his efforts to train them to new ways. Most important, they must continue to reproduce as domesticates. These conditions being fulfilled, men might simply keep control of the movements of their herds and continue to sow a part of the seeds from the crops they harvest. However, the crucial feature of domestication is man's control over the breeding of his domesticates. He improves his crops by sowing only selected seeds and his animals by allowing only those with desirable features to breed. This requires the knowledge that characteristics of plants and animals are passed on to successive generations; few domesticators have failed to understand and take advantage of this fact. It has led to the development of wooly sheep and heavy-headed grains. In fact, many varieties of animals and plants of the same species are adapted to such different environments that extreme varieties of a single species often cannot survive in the same environment.

Man's control of the breeding of his domesticates sometimes becomes so complete that some of them could not survive without his aid. This is especially true of animals that have been bred to be docile and stupid and then cannot protect themselves from wild predators, and of varieties of grain that have been developed with tough stems to retain seeds, which then resist natural sowing by wind and weather. Domesticates depend for life on man, but man himself depends on them. Thus in securing his food supply through agriculture and animal husbandry, man becomes very dependent on his own creations.

Domesticators must care for and, in a broad sense, cultivate the earth itself. Land must be prepared for sowing by hoeing or raking and some attention must be given to the eradication of competing wild plants. Animals must be herded as much as possible so that they do not overgraze an area, killing plants that otherwise would recover and grow to provide new grazing. In dry regions, canals must be dug and natural water courses altered for irrigation. Small barrage dams may be built to store water from occasional rains, and springs may be dug out and improved. From this man gains a notion of the malleability and manipulability not only of the raw materials from which he makes his tools and the plants and animals he domesticates, but also of the earth—the land itself. Man learns that much of the physical environment is amenable to his control and that success in its control means a rich food supply and a correspondingly secure life. He can mold to his desires wood and stone, plants and animals, and overcome to some extent even the imperatives of climate and weather by altering land surfaces and water courses. An expression of major environmental control is the invention of the well. Villages can be established outside the range where natural rainfall is sufficient for agriculture if a water supply is available for irrigation. But even in areas of sufficient rainfall, villages must be located close enough to rivers or springs so that men and animals have water to drink. Once the principles and techniques of well digging are developed, more land is opened to village farming, and more freedom is possible in choosing village sites.

Each group of domesticators, whether it concentrates primarily on village farming or on nomadic pastoralism, is a self-sufficient unit. All the subsistence needs of the group are provided for from their crops and animals and from the immediate environment. Techniques such as skin curing, weaving, and sewing, which occur among advanced hunters and gatherers, are elaborated. Among man's ways of life we have described so far, this is the first that is so successful that it can provide enough food to allow a large increase in population. Although it involves specialized dependence on only a few species of plants and animals, as does the life of hunters and gatherers, the new way is not simply a method for procuring food—hunting and gathering what nature offers—but a method for *producing* food. Agriculture and animal husbandry have been mechanized in modern times, but the basic principles remain the same. Farmers and herdsmen are almost the sole producers of food for human beings today. Modern food supplies are supplemented only to a small degree by products of hunting and gathering—primarily sea animals and wild plants.

The increase in population made possible by more food is paralleled by an increase in density of population made possible by the new techniques of food production that require relatively small plots of land. Such increases in turn make possible more interaction among people—interaction of both a friendly and an antagonistic nature. Friendly interchanges within and among villages can include some trading in both essential and nonessential goods. Trade could develop naturally among newly sedentary peoples who may have roamed over several ecological zones and been exposed to a wide variety of resources before they settled as villagers with limited territory. No man survives through his skill in any particular craft, be it making hoe handles or music, but he can certainly add to the amenities of his life by trading the products of his special abilities. Some obvious antagonistic encounters would be individual theft, group raiding, and warfare among villages. But again, neither the craftsmen nor the warriors would be full-time specialists in these activities. Certain men may have better memories and imaginations for tradition and ritual, and other men may be more adept at measuring, calculating, and recording; but every man must work in the same way as farmers or herdsmen to survive. There is no full-time specialization in non–food-producing work.

Although individuals are not identified by separate craft specializations, since they are all primarily engaged in the same kind of work, there are still various classifications based on age and property holdings. Labor is divided between the sexes, and within each sex there is also division based on age. Young boys often work with their mothers and sisters, learning their jobs. As they grow older, they help their fathers, and then at maturity work as do the other men. But, since some men and some families will inevitably work harder and more shrewdly than others, they will accumulate and maintain larger holdings of land. Such property will pass down hereditary lines in the families and can be enlarged or decreased through marriage. Class distinctions may develop between large and small property holders, but these distinctions will have little impact on the basic social structure of the villages, since the imperatives of hand labor will not allow greatly diverse property holdings. Leadership, however, will probably more often fall to larger property holders in recognition of the fact that those who control a large property must be intelligent and hardworking.

The control the domesticator of plants and animals exerts over the physical environment is control of the basic source of food energy. Plants capture the radiant energy of the sun and reorganize and store it in the production of seeds and vegetable matter. Animals can utilize the stored energy of plants by eating them and their seeds. By domesticating plants, man gains control over the primary food source for animals. By domesticating animals, he gains control over living organisms that eat plants and greatly concentrate the energy they derive in the form of animal protein. Thus man taps the primary source of food energy by controlling plants, and he assures himself high protein food by controlling animals. In the most general sense, domestication allows man to gain indirect control over some of the sun's radiant energy. Through this control he increases his food supply, with the result that he can live longer and reproduce in greater numbers; both of these facts promote further alterations of the physical environment by man.

The invention of domestication permits a way of life which is extremely successful in solving the problem of food procurement for man. Equally important, it promotes the notion in man that he can modify the physical environment at will to serve his own purposes more fully. A culminating expression of the malleability of the earth is the invention of pottery. Clay can be molded into many forms, and many villagers use it to make unfired bricks for buildings and walls. Long before the invention of pottery, men become familiar with the plastic qualities of clay and with the fact that the application of heat or fire can lead to changes in materials. Particularly in cooking, many chemical and physical changes take place which are of great utility to man. Elemental men use fire to form and harden the wooden points of spears and to cook food. The villagers learn that molded clay can be hardened in fire so that vessels can be made that are impervious to insects, small rodents, and water. The control of such an important process of transforming the raw materials of the earth is of parallel importance to the control of plants and animals. The principles of kiln firing are basic to the techniques of metallurgy, which we will discuss in the next chapter, and the alterations of raw materials controlled in these processes spur men to the experimentation that results in modern chemistry and that ultimately gives man much greater control over the physical environment. For all the control the simplest forms of farming and animal husbandry allow—and they are sufficient for changing the face of the earth and altering the worldwide ecological balance— the actual amount of energy controlled by man with these techniques is very small, since all the work he accomplishes is the result of hand labor.

8

THE ADVANCED
FOOD PRODUCER

The way of life organized around simple farming and animal husbandry is extremely stable. Crop failures and other disasters do occur, but the efficiency of food production is such that reserves can be stored for use when production is low. Overall production can be so good, in fact, and storage facilities so well constructed that a surplus, sometimes very large, can be accumulated. Such a surplus permits man to increase his population quite comfortably. Thus, in farming and herding, man not only copes with the physical environment, he masters it to the extent that he can increase his numbers at a geometric rate.

The hard imperatives of the natural supplies of food animals and plants limit the population of hunters and gatherers, no matter how efficient their tools and methods for food procurement. Although there are also limits on how much food can be produced with the new techniques of farming and herding, so much more can be produced that the supply of food alone is no longer an immediately important factor in limiting human numbers. Improved techniques bring not only a great increase in the absolute quantity of food but also a decrease in the number of men necessary to produce the food.

This means that there are more human beings because of stabilized food production, but since relatively fewer of them are needed to maintain the food supply, full-time division of labor is possible. Men not needed for food production can specialize in other endeavors, primarily in the various crafts. This is the basic situation necessary for the development of a way of life both technologically and socially different from that of simple village farmers. This way of life, which depends on *advanced* food production, is just complex enough to be called civilized. Civilization is the adaptation of a large group of people to the physical environment. With respect to the environment, they must cope with problems stemming from their basic needs for protection, nutrition, and reproduction. The problems of protection from the rigors of climate and predators we have taken to be solved essentially by man's prowess as a builder and hunter. Large numbers of people need large quantities of food, which can be provided by advanced techniques of village farming and animal husbandry. The base of civilization, then, is the farming village, which supports the existence of a large number of people.

Food producers mold the land, plants, and animals on which they depend for food. The simplest production techniques are based on hand labor. The advanced food producer utilizes nonhuman sources of power that permit him to complete more work more easily and more quickly than he could by hand. For example, his most basic invention is the animal-drawn plow. Such a plow is a compound tool in two respects. It combines various parts to make a better tool for digging than either a stick or a stone used alone. A plow pulled by a donkey or an ox is a combination of raw materials, molded to man's purposes, with a living organism, also molded to man's purposes—a new level of complexity in tool refinement. In combining material constructions with living organisms, man invents a compound tool that is self-propelling. Man still must guide the tool and keep its parts in working order, but the primary power which motivates the tool in use is not man's, but that of the animal which is a part of the tool. Since donkeys, oxen, and other draft animals are much stronger than man, using them as sources of power greatly increases the amount of work men can accomplish.

The new level of complexity, then, involves combining the working parts of a tool with a power source other than man, which can still be directed by man. Animals are an obvious source. Plants, though they could certainly be planted in cracks in stones, for example, so that their growth eventually would split the stones, grow too slowly to be of much use. Fire can be used to split stones. Another force that can easily be harnessed, but is not often used, is the pressure exerted by freezing water. Stones can be split by pouring water in cracks and allowing it to freeze. In these instances, plants, fire, and water or ice would be self-propelling simple tools, exerting natural forces directed by man to achieve a specific purpose.

Increased production necessitates an increase in transportation of food products to storage places. Around bodies of water, the use of boats with sails makes transportation easier and faster. Greater efficiency and ease in land transportation is accomplished through the use of animals. Materials to be carried can be piled on their backs or placed on sledges to be pulled behind them. But the most important improvement on hauling techniques is the wheel, the most versatile of man's mechanical inventions. Man learns very quickly that if friction is minimal, it is easier to push or pull an object up an inclined plane than it is to lift it straight up, and it becomes increasingly easier the lower the angle of the inclined plane. A wheel utilizes the principle of the inclined plane; attached to a container to be pulled or pushed along the ground, it is, in effect, a perpetual inclined plane. The mechanical advantage enjoyed is proportional to the diameter of the wheel, for a large wheel forms a smaller angle with the ground than a small wheel.

With the wheel, advanced food producers were able to exploit two other sources of power: wind and flowing water. Mills powered by the energy of wind or flowing water can exert great force, which can be used for grinding, drilling, sawing, and many other purposes. These inanimate sources of power, when combined with the working parts of a tool, may represent a lower level of complexity than do compound tools that utilize animal power. However, the basic principle of the self-propelled tool is the same. Wind and flowing water are joined with the working materials in the tool to provide a driving force that is guided by man to work for his specific purposes.

Even more important than its use in production and transportation of men and food supplies are those uses of the wheel, particularly in the form of gears, for the development of tools and techniques for mass production of manufactured goods. However, given an increased demand for manufactured goods because of a larger population, mass-production techniques in the crafts must be invented to produce satisfactory quantities. Two illustrations are sufficient to show the utility of the wheel in the development of such techniques. Clay pots can be made by hand either by molding them from solid pieces of clay or by building them up with successive rings of rolled clay. Such methods are slow, and products become standardized only after the potter has attained great skill. However, if a horizontal disk can be made to spin rapidly, a lump of clay placed in the center can be molded with the hands and fingers as it spins around with the wheel. In this way standard pottery forms can be produced rapidly with much less time spent by the potter for each pot produced. A second important use of the wheel in crafts is the spinning wheel, which, after several transformations and elaborations, is incorporated into textile factories, powered in some cases, by the energy of running water.

The technological advances made possible by exploitation of nonhuman sources of power permit a large increase in population and full-time occupational specializations, which are essential social features of civilized society. To see how these features are related, let us first consider population growth. In a simple farming situation, everyone does more or less the same work. Vast numbers of people can be supported with simple farming techniques; for example, in rice farming, tons of grain can be produced from a relatively small acreage. As farmland becomes occupied, the density of farmers will increase along with the increasing population. But since farmers are generally self-sufficient, they have little reason to travel beyond their own villages or to trade among themselves. There is no reason for them to have contact with strangers, unless they must go to war against them to protect their property. Society might remain village- and kinship-oriented, even with great populations.

However, there is good reason for supposing that this type of society is unlikely to develop in actuality, since in most environments it would take many generations before the human population reached such proportions that there would be enough food produced for everyone only if everyone were engaged in farming. Advanced food-producing techniques make it possible for just a few men to produce enough food for many. Consequently, a significant proportion of the village inhabitants can specialize in occupations other than farming and herding. Increased production of food by fewer workers is closely related to the development of craft specializations.

Full-time division of labor, with different men producing more of various products than they themselves can use, and at the same time not producing many products that they do need, means that the society must have some form of exchange of goods. In small village communities the redistribution of goods can be along kinship lines or across these lines, according to utility and need. If specialization leads to mass production, and if the products thus become so numerous that they can be disposed of through trade beyond the village or local community, then civilized social institutions must be developed to expedite these matters. Villagers who produce more food and manufactured goods than they themselves can consume, and who trade these products to consumers with whom they do not have day-to-day, face-to-face contact or to middlemen, are the backbone of a civilization. Trading brings about two further occupational specializations: merchant-middlemen, who pass goods from producer to consumer, and merchant-carriers, who transport goods from place to place.

The primary social consequence of this proliferation of food and manufactured products is a weakening of the social structure based on kinship and a strengthening of class ties across kinship lines. The increase in population and goods is accompanied by an increase in wealth. Class differentiations develop between the rich and the poor, between landowners or factory proprietors and workers. They also develop along occupational lines. The simplest reason for these class divisions is utility; they facilitate necessary interactions among people.

An increase in wealth gives rise to three new occupational classifications: priests to conduct ritual celebrations of wealth and its vicissitudes, soldiers to protect or expropriate property, and clerks to keep records and make calculations. Because of their specialized functions, priests, soldiers, and clerks are in a position to set standards of behavior and to regularize codes of conduct. It is from one or the other of these classes, therefore, that leaders or kings of cities or states are likely to arise. This is not to say that rich men are unlikely to become rulers. They are much more likely to become rulers, however, if they have in addition to riches the knowledge, authority, and prestige of a priest, a general, or a clerical scholar or politician. A very powerful leader may impose his will on the direction of the economy of a large region, occupying some areas with his armies and exacting tribute from the inhabitants and protecting other areas with his armies at the price of taxes imposed on the inhabitants.

Large cities are not essential for civilization, but the ease of interaction they permit among many people makes it very likely that cities will develop. Such cities may often be composed of tens of thousands of people, none of whom is in the business of primary food production. Their food is usually supplied by farmers in villages surrounding the city, but in some cases may be imported from hundreds of miles away. The villagers, in turn, may depend on tools, clothes, and other goods manufactured in the city. Villagers who are so dependent on their interaction with the city are called peasants. Villagers who are bound by the power of local kings or landowners are called serfs, and those who are themselves the property of a private owner or of the state are slaves.

The intricate control the city or state structure exerts upon the production and distribution of food and goods both necessitates and makes possible a further occupational specialization. Raw materials must be procured and transported to villages that specialize in making products from them or to factories in the cities. Thus, communities are formed around specific tasks, such as mining and logging. The people in these villages exchange the raw materials they produce for food and manufactured goods. The demand for certain raw materials may lead to long-distance trade and the production of goods to be used primarily for trade.

Large numbers of people of different occupational specialties living close to one another in a city interact with one another on a qualitatively different level from that of farmers in a small village. In village society, everyone knows everyone else, and almost all interactions are face-to-face. In the city, the citizen knows only a few of his fellows. Many of his relations with other citizens are through middlemen, and many of the goods he needs and obtains are produced by individuals either within or outside the city with whom he has no direct contact. He may have only the vaguest notion of how his food is produced and how it is transported and traded until it reaches his hands. In such situations, however, someone must know and oversee the channels of interaction and communication among individuals who do not see or contact one another directly. A centralized coordinating agency seems necessary. A large population of specialists necessitates trade, and trade in turn requires centralization.

Such centralization may be established on kinship. However, even a greatly extended family line is not the most efficient struc-

large pop of specialist → trade → centralization

ture on which to organize occupational specialization and the redistribution of goods. More commonly, occupational class lines are established that cut across kinship lines. People who coordinate trade
are thus likely to come from the class of merchants and traders who
are middlemen between producers and consumers and who understand the needs and behavior of both these groups.

Besides the economic institution, two other affiliations that cut
across kinship lines can attain importance in civilized society. Religious organizations with priests as leaders in matters of moral codes
not only can bypass kinship relations but also can cut across occupational class lines. Citizen allegiance to an army composed of a small
body of professional soldiers can be extensive, and in wartime, citizen soldiers from all ranks of society may submit to rigid central
control. Overriding all these broad institutional ties—to family,
occupational class, religion, and army—is the universal tie of all individuals to the city, or more properly the state, which includes the
city (or cities) and all outlying areas in its (or their) sphere of control or influence. Broadly speaking, the primary affiliation of the
civilized man is with the state.

Centralized authority for the state itself may come from the
family leadership of great property-holders, from the hierarchy of
religious leaders, or from the generals of the army. It may also—in
effect, if not in name—come from a specialized clerical class that
is required to service the record-keeping needs of rulers. Leaders
from each of these groups necessarily have some controlling influence over various essential institutions; a strong leader in one sphere
of activity may extend his influence over other institutions, perhaps
becoming in time absolute ruler of the state. A much more detailed
presentation would be necessary to show the conditions in which it
would be likely that the leadership of a state would come from the
religious rather than the military hierarchy, for example. It is our
purpose merely to elaborate slightly the broad generalization that
for nonchaotic interaction among individuals in a large group of

people, some centralized controlling authority is needed in order to have what can be called a civilized state.

Centralized leadership can be made more effective by the codification of both moral and economic regulations. To unify such codes, religious and civil leadership may be combined. The military may be involved, also, to impose sanctions. In effect, the leaders thus become legislators, and their legislation gives rise to new occupational classes. Lawyers and judges, as well as policemen, are necessary to interpret and mediate the civil law.

The rulers of the state may be the only individuals in the society who have enough centralized power to accomplish very large construction projects, such as those involving monumental architecture and extensive canal systems for irrigation or transport. To command the money and labor for such projects, taxation is often imposed. Some taxation may be thought necessary just to support the ordinary activities of civil servants. For great construction projects, rulers may impress their own subjects or send their armies on missions of conquest to procure slaves as well as material riches.

Imperialism may arise out of the need or the desire for more workers, more territory, more natural resources, or more taxes. It may also be part of a desire to spread one's own culture. The imperialistic mission, in broad terms, is an attempt to impose standardization on a large body of people over a large area. Such standardization is essential to harmonious economic interactions. If products and exchange rates are standardized within a state, then many difficulties are avoided. For example, the imposition by rulers of a single state language, a single state religion, and standardized devices for exchange, such as coinage, not only makes human interactions easier but also unifies the citizens of the state. What they have in common —their language, their customs, and the territory of the state—are the elements of a basic affiliation that cuts across all others, and particularly across the lines of kinship.

A crucial element for the efficient operation of a state is writing.

Written records are the heart of any large-scale regulatory organization. Writing enables the merchant and trader to keep track of a multitude of transactions and inventories without having to rely on memory. Rulers can keep records of their property and of the credits and debits of taxation. Moral and economic codes can be established in explicit terms for all (literate) men to see. Civil law can be recorded in books. Most important, however, writing permits the cumulation and cultural transmission of knowledge on a scale that is impossible as long as men must rely on memory and the spoken word. Advances of knowledge can be recorded in a form that is very nearly permanent in comparison with oral tradition. Mathematicians and geometers, for example, are necessary to take measurements and make calculations in the construction of large buildings and canals; the advent of written quantitative records makes possible mathematical astronomy, which in turn leads to the immense advances of mathematical physics. Writing, used in the most elementary way, provides an efficient means of keeping the records and coordinating the affairs of a civilized state, both of which could be done only with difficulty without writing. Writing, used in the most advanced way, is a creative instrument of modern science, which could not be undertaken without it.

On a more abstract level, the civilized way of life described here embodies the codification of space and time. The seasons and territories important to hunters and gatherers do not need to be measured very exactly. Measurement does become more important to domesticators as they keep track of their animals and crops. But work is done when it needs to be done and is tallied in terms of progress and completion rather than in terms of time and amount. In the civilized state, factory production puts a premium on the measure of unit output of product as well as on time taken for production. Taxes are exacted in amounts of goods or time periods of work. Men who do not work solely for themselves must measure their work not in terms of need but in terms of output and time spent. The codification of temporal and material matters is a result of the need to standardize the complex interactions of a large number of people.

The influence of the civilized state can extend far beyond its own territory. New mathematical skills can be used in the art of navigation; sailing ships can be constructed to take advantage of the motive power of the wind; metallurgy can be developed to provide durable, intricate, and efficient tools; and factories can be powered by the force of steam escaping from boiling water confined in heated tanks. The production of goods for trade to distant lands can make the influence of a civilized society worldwide. However, such influence at bottom continues to depend on the food-production base.

Civilized societies are often said to have overcome the imperatives of the physical environment, but this is true only in the sense that some individuals and some communities, by being part of a larger integrated organization, the state, can devote themselves to activities that are not directly related to providing protection or producing food. They exchange their products for protection and food provided by other groups within the state. It is still necessary for the state as a whole to be in ecological balance with the physical environment, but because of intensive food production on the part of a few and because of efficient methods of exchange of goods, not everyone in the state need be directly concerned with coping with the environment. Thus, parts of the society may appear to be living out of balance with nature, but it is a deception to believe that any large group of men can live as a total organization out of balance with nature successfully for very long.

9 | INDUSTRIAL MAN

As Chapters 6–8 show, the more people there are interacting, the more complex and varied the interactions are likely to be. This variety and complexity ultimately require a coordinating, centralized control. And as centralization makes possible more control, more control makes possible centralization in more areas. Society's growth potential, as well as that of institutions within it, is related to the ability of leaders to influence large numbers of people indirectly through a small manageable number of people over whom they have direct control. A hierarchical pyramid of administrators and managers is one organizational structure in which this is possible: it allows leaders at the top of the pyramid to maintain face-to-face relations with key subordinates in the hierarchy. This pyramidal social arrangement is an efficient solution to many of the organizational problems of government and economics among advanced food producers, and it is an essential structure for a society as large as that of the industrial state. The relationship of factory owner, worker, and consumer reflects this kind of structure: factory owners have indirect influence on large numbers of people through their direct control over a limited number of workers. In a modern factory, a relatively small number of workers (considering the number of prospective consumers) can produce a large quantity of goods—goods whose number and type may be determined by as few as one or two men. Their choices directly influence the labor of the factory workers and indirectly influence the lives of great numbers of consumers. This kind of broad control can be exercised where industrialization has expanded beyond the limited factory arrangements—for pottery, textiles, weapons, and other small goods —described in Chapter 8, which rely on the steam engine, powered by wood or, more efficiently, charcoal fires. Industrialization could not expand greatly, however, without the use of fossil fuels to provide large amounts of energy in concentrated forms.

Coal, oil, and natural gas are fossil residues from organic materials deposited and incorporated as a part of the geologic strata in the remote past. Most of the coal and oil deposits that make industrialization possible are at least two hundred million years old. The energy they concentrate is stored solar energy, fixed in organic matter by the photosynthetic activity of green plants. Consequently, by utilizing these fossil fuels, man is again using solar energy and is dependent on the activity of plants to concentrate this energy in a form he can use.

In every way of life, tools are designed for what man recognizes as available energy sources. The weapons of advanced hunters and gatherers, for example, are geared to the energy output of the human body alone. Animal-drawn plows are adjusted to the amount of energy that can be exerted by donkeys and oxen. Before fossil fuels can be employed effectively, there must be machines capable of converting this kind of fuel into power. The most elementary of such machines is the steam engine. Wood-burning models can be improved and modified for use with coal and oil. Coal- and oil-burning machines can turn out immense quantities of usable power, greatly exceeding that of machines propelled by water or by wood fires. For the development of advanced machines that burn fossil fuels, the art of metallurgy must be adequate to the production of large metal tanks and machine parts.

Industrialization brings about a variety of occupational specializations; large communities of miners are necessary, for example, and since raw materials—fossil fuels and mineral ores—are often geographically separated from one another and from factories, a large-scale transport system is required. All these specialists—miners, transporters, metallurgists, and machinists—most of whom have nothing directly to do with food production, must be fed. Thus, the basic material foundation of industrial development is the food surplus made possible by the advanced food-producing techniques discussed in the last chapter.

Industrialization enables man to do more than just cope with the natural environment. Industrial man has great control over nature. He does not simply survive or even just flourish grandly; he takes the earth in hand and molds it to his wishes. He develops various techniques for using the materials of the earth that go far beyond the modifications of the natural environment that are necessary to solve the elementary problems of protection, nutrition, and reproduction. Industrial man succeeds so well in taking care of these needs that he can greatly elaborate his basic tools for survival and can manufacture many products that are completely nonessential. He can, of course, through conditioning become psychologically dependent on some of these so-called nonessential products; but our concern is primarily with material culture and man's direct relationship with the physical environment, and a discussion of such possible psychological developments is beyond the scope of this book.

With the discovery of the use of fossil fuels, large areas of invention are opened to engineers and machinists. A ruler of an elementary civilized state might conceive of a great building or canal system, but it would take a lifetime and the labor of multitudes of men and animals to execute his plan. Modern engineers with new energy sources complete in a few years the construction of dams and buildings of giant dimensions. The mother of invention may in some part be necessity, but the limits of invention are largely set by the amounts of raw materials and utilizable energy available. The three increasingly complex human ways of life described in Chapters 8–10 depend in each case on the discovery of new sources of energy. The first is made possible by the domestication of plants and animals and by the exploitation of natural forces, such as wind and water; the second, by the utilization of fossil fuels; and the third, by the harnessing of atomic energy. Industrialization allows man to master many natural forces in the environment and to remake much of the world according to his own plans. The invention of more efficient and diverse methods and machines permits production of larger and larger quantities and varieties of food and manufactured goods. Over great areas of the earth large-scale farming and herding cause a shift from the natural ecology, often quite complex and varied, to the simplified ecology of food-producing man. For hundreds of species of plants and animals, man substitutes a few domesticated species. Over-grazing by sheep and goats and plowing year after year can lead to loss of plants and to erosion, leaving virtual desert waste in the place of once fertile lands. Intensive irrigation can result in salt deposits in the soil that make agriculture impossible. By extracting raw materials for manufacturing man also alters the environment: deforested mountains and strip-mined prairies must adjust to new ecological balances determined by man's activities.

In making the world over, man not only causes large-scale modifications but also becomes dependent on them. The vast quantities of food and manufactured goods will remain surplus unless the population grows enough to use them, so industrialization is most often accompanied by a large increase in population. The only natural limit to industrial expansion is that of producible food and goods. It will, therefore, most likely expand until all possible farmlands and sources of raw materials are utilized.

As we have seen, industrialization depends not only on the presence of a source of high-level energy but also on the scientific and engineering knowledge that enables man to use it. This depends, in turn, on the development of modern mathematics. Mathematics is a science that cannot be pursued or taught at any level of complexity or sophistication without some form of writing. The advance of knowledge in part depends, then, on the development of writing.

The physical manifestation of writing consists of visible marks that have standardized forms and meanings. Such marks are intended to have specific meaning by the men who make them, for the purpose of communication with others or with themselves at a later time. The simplest forms of writing are mnemonic devices—devices calculated to aid a person in remembering. Making marks to count or record the numbers of things is an example of such a simple form of writing. Writing of wider use can develop out of the art of realistic drawing. Pictographic writing utilizes pictures to convey meaning similar to what is pictured. As long as the pictures are identifiable, the intention to communicate is understood, and if the message is fairly simple, pictographic writing can be understood universally by men who speak different languages. The marks or pictures used are symbolic of their meanings, and in the cases given above, resemble their referents in some respect. Such marks are therefore called ikonic symbols.

Once the notion is understood, most intelligent human beings can understand simple pictographic writing. However, its utility is fairly limited, so more versatile forms of writing are invented. Ideographic writing is composed of arbitrarily chosen marks, each of which symbolizes a different idea. Since the meanings of the symbols are arbitrarily established, one must learn what each symbol means. The value of ideographic writing is also limited, however, since a huge number of ideographs—too many for most men to memorize and use with facility—is required for all the possible topics of communication.

The most versatile form of writing utilizes symbols that neither picture the objects intended nor stand for the ideas meant but that represent the phonemes of human speech. Since most human languages have fewer than several hundred phonemes, the phonemographic system of writing can employ a limited alphabet, one or a combination of letters representing each phoneme of the spoken language. These letters can then be put together into written words. Just as the phonemes of human speech do not in themselves have meanings but morphemes, composed of phonemes, do, so individual letters do not have meanings, but words composed from them do. The important convention governing the meaning of written words is that they symbolize the same meanings as do the morphemes with which they are coordinated. If one sounds out the phonemes represented by the letters making up a written word, one makes a sound that has a specific meaning. In this way, a limited number of letters can be combined to make an unlimited number of words. Phonemographic writing has exactly the same degree of versatility as spoken language. With an extensive phonemographic alphabet, one can write down words of any human language.

Whatever can be conveyed through spoken language, then, can be written. We have already discussed some of the implications of this fact for economics and government in the last chapter. The advantages written language provides for the advancement of knowledge should be obvious. Teaching need no longer be face-to-face by oral transmission, and what is learned need no longer be retained by memory alone. Human knowledge is always cumulative, with the experience of ancestors being passed on from generation to generation. Writing makes possible the storage of knowledge too intricate to be carried easily in the minds of men. In a library a student has access to bodies of knowledge no single mind would or could retain. In a sense, writing is still a mnemonic device; however, its most important use is not in storing knowledge for the writer but in making this knowledge immediately available to other men.

The use of written symbols is essential to the development of mathematics. Some men are capable of doing intricate mathematical calculations in their heads, but most men need the aid of written symbols to keep the order of their mathematical investigations. The most important development from written mathematics is mathematical physics. Problems in plane and solid geometry can be described with pictographic symbols, but they can also be represented with algebraic formulas. With the invention of analytic geometry, which relates the ideographic writing of algebra to the pictographic writing of geometry, come new powers of describing static physical objects in mathematical terms. With the invention of the differential and integral calculus, which makes possible the description of continuous events, come new powers of describing dynamic physical objects in mathematical terms. These inventions in mathematics, with the realization that mathematical calculi can be used to describe physical phenomena, are what make possible all the advances of modern physics.

Writing makes possible not only the advance of knowledge but also the wide dissemination of ideas of all sorts. A literate population can, for example, be permitted, induced, or compelled to read the same religious or political tracts and in the process become standardized in their ideological beliefs. Rulers who have control of the written word have a tool of great value in unifying the people of their realm; with it they can excite religious fervor, patriotic zeal, and devotion to causes. However, though it is important to the processes of further centralization and control, the written word can be superseded by means of communication powered by electricity. Papers can be printed and transported quickly by modern means, but they still must be distributed and read. The discovery of electricity makes possible long-distance and mass-communication apparatus. With the telegraph and telephone, the wireless radio and television, a message can be communicated just as rapidly as words can be spoken, and radio and television make possible the immediate presentation of the same message to millions of people all over the world.

As mechanical tools for molding ideas, radio and television are two of man's most effective inventions. It seems probable that whatever religious or political ideas are approved and widely disseminated by those in power in a large society will be ideas that will in some way further their aims. The most acceptable ideas, in other words, will be those that further development of the society along lines conceived by those in power. The rulers will influence the production of artists and writers as well. Rulers will not necessarily be infallible, nor will they be either completely benevolent or totally vicious. The absolute sway of deviant, radical, and rebellious ideas is as unlikely as is their total absence. We can be sure, however, that, whatever the ideas disseminated, the leadership will make use of every available instrument for communication as a means of centralizing control over the varied and complex industrial society.

The great increase in population and production that industrialization makes possible has already been presented as the grounds for greater complexity and centralization of human relations. The degree of complexity involved can be seen in the increased occupational specialization in modern factories that makes possible greatly increased efficiency of production. Where workers may have once made complete chairs, for example, many more chairs can be constructed if one man makes the legs, another the seats, and so on, and still other workers put the pieces together. Assembly-line methods often specialize the workingman's labor to minute tasks. This increased mechanization makes necessary an economic system in which money is the medium of exchange. Whether the means of production are owned and managed by private individuals or by the state, the extensive redistribution of goods that is required is best effected through standardized values set in monetary terms. Very few workers receive any amount of their production as compensation for the work they do; instead they receive wages according to the amount of piecework they turn out or the length of time they spend on the job. Thus, specific measurements—of time, money, and materials—are very important to industrial man.

Rulers of industrial states have control over masses of men, and they can exercise and strengthen this power through writing, radio, and television. Their power is also apparent in the control they exert on the economic and productive processes. Workers can be employed or not, market prices can be manipulated, and taxes can be set; thus the worker, the consumer, and the citizen (considered as parts of the physical environment) are as much in the control of man as are the other essential materials for industrialization. The extent of this control is no better illustrated than by the mobilization of a large state for war. The means of instantaneous communication are utilized both to coordinate the mobilization and to convince the masses of its necessity. Industry is brought under tight central control, with coordination between units that in peacetime may have been competitors. And, most basic, supplies of food are closely controlled, often by rationing. Thus, the success of industrialization depends on an organization of elements which permits integration to the degree that one central agency can take control of the entire structure of society.

The industrial state, then, provides a way of life in which man copes with and interacts with the physical environment, employing tools, machines, and institutions geared to the utilization of high levels of energy from fossil fuels. Man is literally capable of moving mountains, for he has control of most aspects of the physical environment. Through scientific advance, he learns to convert the energy of fossil fuels into versatile chemical and electrical energy. Once ways of using electricity are invented, the forces of wind and water can be turned to its generation. A most important use of electricity is for mass communication, since in the industrial state men must themselves be controlled. Widespread, effective, and centralized control can be exerted by the force of armies in simple civilized states, but highly efficient control depends on writing and widespread literacy and on such means of mass communication as radio and television. The most distinctive aspect of the industrial way of life is that its success necessitates subjecting men as well as materials to large-scale manipulation and centralized control and that a new technology is developed for molding men as well as materials.

The large population of the industrial state does not depend entirely on increased efficiency in food production. One of man's greatest enemies is disease, about which we have said little because in none of the ways of life described so far are there any effective ways of contending with it. It must be accepted, along with the composition of the air man breathes to maintain life, as one of the constant factors of the physical environment. As men group together and have more contact with one another in farm villages and cities, disease becomes a more serious problem and takes a larger toll of lives. Only with the great scientific advances of industrial society can medicine be developed sufficiently to provide real and extensive protection from disease. The special instruments and techniques and large-scale production of pure chemicals and compounds for medicines depend on industrial processes. Once simple methods of disease control such as immunization are discovered and put into effect on a large scale, the result is a greater increase in population than that engendered by increased food production. Men reproduce slowly in comparison to other animals, and their uncontrolled birth rate is probably about the same in any of the ways of life we have described so far, but more effective ways of contending with the natural environment mean a decrease in the death rate. The flourishing of medicine in industrial society cuts the death rate drastically, especially among infants. Increased food may be responsible for increased population after the invention of farming and herding, but the greatly increased population of industrial society is largely a result of medical inventions.

The consequences of industrial development are not all beneficial to man, however. The burning of fossil fuels increases the amounts of dust, carbon, carbon dioxide, and various complex chemical compounds in the atmosphere, with potentially harmful physical effects on man. With the advent of internal combustion machines, large quantities of carbon monoxide and other compounds are added to the atmosphere. These combustion wastes often combine in highly dangerous compounds, collectively called smog, which pollute the atmosphere to some degree over every large city in the industrialized world. Not only the air men breathe but also the water they drink is polluted with industrial and household wastes to such a degree that almost all water for drinking in industrial society must be purified by adding to it minute amounts of poison to kill bacteria dangerous to man. Numerous chemical preservatives and adulterants are added to foods that must be transported long distances, and numerous insecticides and other poisons are used in the production of plants and animals for human food. The human organism is changed by the medicines used to ward off and combat disease, and by the caffeine, nicotine, alcohol, and other narcotic drugs, which man probably consumes at all levels of life so far described.

Industrial man is not merely a part of nature, but a part of *controlled* nature, that is, a part of the physical environment over which man has gained immense control. A step beyond is atomic man, who, through his discovery of a virtually unlimited source of energy, has such powerful control of nature that he can change both men and materials in almost all those mythical ways attributed to the gods, except for changing the laws of nature themselves.

10

ATOMIC MAN

Although our descriptions of ways of life are syntheses derived from analysis of the data of paleontology, ethology, archeology, ethnology, and history, the protohuman way of life is, necessarily, a construction based primarily on logic. The way of life of atomic man must be based on equally speculative grounds. We are living in an age of atomic energy, but so little of its potential has yet been actualized that our way of life is still basically that of industrial, not atomic, man. If the description of the protohuman way of life can be viewed as an attempt to construct what might have been, then the description of the way of life of atomic man can be considered an attempt to predict what might be. Each description, of course, can stand on its own as a possible way of life developing from physical and social conditions existing in earlier ways of life.

Industrial man uses a new energy source—fossil fuels—to further the accomplishments of the elementary civilized state. Most of the differences between the two ways of life are expressed not in any particularly novel attacks on the physical environment, but in the increased centralization of ruling power, which makes possible more extensive and tighter control over man himself, and in the rapid population growth, encouraged by a surplus of food and goods and made possible by the spectacular achievements of medical science.

Although men could reproduce to the limit of the world's food supply, power differences on an international scale are apt to prevent them from doing so. Industrial development and centralization lead to class distinctions between owners and workers, rich and poor, and rulers and ruled, and these are paralleled worldwide with rich and powerful industries and nations controlling and benefiting from the actions of weak and poor industries and nations. Thus, one or a few nations can dominate all the others. Such domination is most important for integrated economics and for efficiency in warfare, which in many cases breaks out because of the imperatives of this or that economic structure. Entire nations can be relegated by mercantile policies to the role of supplier of raw materials and consumer under control of the nation that produces most of the manufactured goods. Since raw materials have value only when they are needed for production, the nation controlling the factories will usually become—because of its commanding position—rich and powerful. And because of this dichotomous class power structure, the population can be held at a level lower than the food base can support, and the more powerful men and nations can consume more of the world's food and goods than is necessary for their adequate protection, nutrition, and reproduction. In the process of assuring themselves this luxury they actually deprive other nations and people of food and goods adequate to their basic needs. This disparity may in fact be dictated by the economic, political, or social structure of the ruling nation or the major manufacturing and business institutions within it, and it may be necessary to maintain it in order to protect the economic and political stability of the ruling nation.

The social institutions of the industrial state are exploitative; its technology is extractive. This technology depends on mining the resources of the earth and distributing the products made from them in nonrecoverable, nonreusable ways. The industrial way of life will last only as long as both the fossil fuels that provide the energy and the raw materials in concentrations that can be refined with such levels of energy are available. When these sources have been exhausted, man will have to revert, perhaps, to an elementary civilized way of life or to farming villages. The problem the physical environment sets for industrial society, then, is that of developing a technology which will permit a balance between the raw materials men use and the reusable material and organic wastes of man. Such a balance is approximated on a small scale where farmers grow grain to feed animals and then return manure to the soil as fertilizer. Such an ecological balance is demanded in man's relationship with the physical environment if he—like any other animal in the ecological community—is to survive. Industrial man may not be in danger of destroying his habitat to such an extent that men can maintain no way of life, but he is in explicit danger of extracting and using raw materials from the earth in such a way that he will ultimately make the industrial way of life impossible.

The harnessing of atomic energy presents man with two possibilities: abundance or extinction. Atomic energy is released in a chain reaction of explosions. Controlled explosive combustion is employed in an industrial society, in internal combustion engines, for example, and explosives themselves are of great use for mining and construction. Explosives are also employed effectively in war, and since the simplest way to release atomic energy on a large scale is in the form of large explosions, it is likely that the use of atomic energy will first be as an explosive weapon in war. Atomic weapons are very powerful, and the intense heat they generate causes fire storms over any city on which they are dropped, resulting in immense losses in property and human life. But of greater danger is the radioactive material, deadly to man, which is released in the atmosphere, where it is distributed around the world by the wind. Levels of radiation that are fatal to all men, or even to all life on earth, can result from large-scale warfare or simply from large-scale testing of atomic weapons in the atmosphere. However, through the intelligent use of the vast amount of energy provided by man's control of atomic fission, a technology of equilibrium can be developed, making possible the egalitarian satisfaction of the basic human needs for all men. The development of a technology of equilibrium, which establishes a recycling use of raw materials, is essential to the establishment of civilized industrial society on a basis that will support man through the millions of years of his biological potential.

Industrialization as a way of life does not cease with the utilization of atomic energy. What the new source of energy allows is a proliferation of industrialization on an almost unlimited scale and in unlimited directions. Given the understanding of ecologic systems provided by modern science, and realizing that the earth as a whole is an ecologic system in which man must live in balance, intelligent men can utilize atomic energy to develop a technology in which the materials used for production are recycled for unlimited reuse. With the prospect of sufficient energy available, men may be able to invent processes for synthesizing from ordinary materials, such as sea water and granite, everything needed for modern industrial manufacturing. Even food can be produced through the reorganization of matter made possible by the availability of atomic energy and the scientific advances it fosters. Thus, by expanding drastically the number and variety of food sources and by providing techniques for adapting and conserving raw materials for industry, atomic technology can make possible a comfortable living for all men, and in doing so may tend to resolve the power differences among nations of the world.

The radioactive energy that supports the industries of atomic man, though it may in fact derive ultimately from the sun, since all the material of the earth may originally have been part of the sun's mass, is the first form of energy we have discussed that does not derive directly or indirectly from the actual radiant energy of the sun. With the harnessing of atomic energy, man might conceivably live on earth without using any of the radiant energy of the sun.

However, it is likely that in time solar radiation will provide even more energy for man than does atomic fission, since readily fissionable materials are limited on earth, just as are other raw materials. The largest and most long-term source of energy available to man is the radiant energy of the sun, and it will probably be the source of energy for man's ultimate harmonic ecological adjustment to what will in all probability be an earth remade by man. Two great advantages of solar radiation as a source of energy are that it does not wastefully dissipate the valuable organic compounds of fossil fuels and that it does not distribute dangerous radioactive wastes.

Atomic man can remake the earth into forms that appear more congenial to him than natural circumstances. The first worldwide controls to be effected are most probably those over climate and weather. In time the entire ecological community may be remade, since it is most efficient for man to control all plant and animal interactions on earth. The patterns of land and sea can also be changed on a large scale. In effect, all species and the earth itself are finally domesticated by atomic man.

The most important object of atomic man's reconstruction is man himself. In all the ways of life described so far man alters his constitution by the use of drugs; industrial man is subject to further man-made changes from industrial wastes in the atmosphere and water, food additives, insecticides, and medicines. Atomic man adds radioactive elements to these influences. All these have actual or potential influence on human genetic structure. In particular, medicine makes possible the survival and reproduction of many human beings who are physically or mentally defective in some way and who would not survive or reproduce without medicine. Radioactivity causes direct mutations of the genes. The general level of protection provided by modern society, in fact, makes likely the survival of many more defective human beings than in more stringent ways of life and thus the perpetuation of their weaknesses among men. The hierarchical social structure also has effects: large parts of certain populations may be continuously undernourished or overfed; imprudent men may reproduce at a higher rate than their more prudent or more intelligent fellows. Psychological stress from the tensions of overcrowding or the high mobility made possible by modern means of transportation and occupational variety may also have effects on men's health and physical constitution. Men who travel halfway around the world in a few hours suffer for several days from physiological disruptions of their circadian, or daily, rhythms, and men who change from job to job may suffer from loss of identification with any permanent human community.

Men are aware of these influences and of their results. The logical step is to employ them intentionally to produce men of desirable physical and mental constitutions. We have already discussed one such mass change that results from the discovery of medical means to control the infectious diseases that are so destructive to men living in large groups. Vaccines prevent people from catching various diseases and suffering physical or mental impairment. Another massive change is in the treatment of diseases and in the prolongation of the lives of many people who suffer from serious disruptions of their organic parts. Hormonic birth-control methods can be used to alter and control the natural rhythms of the body. The impetus for this development is most likely to come from the threat of overpopulation. With the discovery of the genetic code and further understanding of the construction of the human body and all its parts, major genetic and physical readjustments can be made in the nature of man. At this level of knowledge, man's control of nature extends to the entire physical environment and includes not only behavioral but also genetic control of man himself. In some circumstances this can lead to better physical and mental health for almost everyone except a few statistical failures; in other circumstances it can lead to slavery for the masses or to the extinction of man as a result of biological warfare.

We have already seen that the way of life of industrial man depends on his technology and that his technology in turn depends on the availability of energy sources and raw materials. Once these materials are exhausted, the way of life must change. The advanced industrial way of life—the way of life of atomic man—is based on a technology that through recycling of materials permits man to perpetuate such a level indefinitely. Atomic technology is the most successful instrument for coping with and modifying the physical environment. Obviously, atomic man is more permanently dependent on his technology for his mere existence than is man in any of the simpler ways of life we have described. His dependence may, in fact, be irreversible. It is possible for atomic man to remake the world and to remold his own constitution in such a way that without the perpetuation of his technology he could not survive on earth. The advanced technology and the scientific knowledge it implies are immensely versatile. Man can colonize the planets of his solar system. He can meet emergencies, perhaps even on the scale of the sun's growing cold or the moon's plunging into the earth. He may even be able to remake himself into an organism with gills capable of living under water. But what he cannot do—once he has adjusted himself to the intricacies of the atomic way of life through genetic alteration—is survive the sudden loss of his technology. The point we are stressing here, then, is that the most successful method possible for coping with the physical environment is one that makes man completely dependent on it. His technical skill makes him capable of controlling great parts of the physical environment. But because he simplifies the world's ecological system and because simpler ecological systems are more vulnerable to upset than are complex systems, man makes his culture as a whole much more vulnerable to overthrow by catastrophe than the cultures of ways of life that do not alter the natural ecology of the world so much.

One problem remains which atomic technology alone cannot solve: for the first time, man's basic need to reproduce becomes a problem—not the problem of reproducing in sufficient numbers, but the problem of avoiding overpopulation. Not until the atomic level is reached is the energy base so large that the provision of adequate food and manufactured goods for a vast population is very easily possible. But even here there is a limit. The earth is still a finite system on which there is enough space and material for only so many human beings. It is probable that even with the production made possible by the use of atomic energy, men will reproduce to intolerable numbers unless something other than lack of sufficient food curbs them. Intelligent men can utilize the knowledge available about the earth as an ecologic system to determine what size population is most compatible with human life of a given quality, supported by the food and product base provided by the technology of equilibrium. Of course, the decision as to what constitutes the desired level of quality must be worked out between the rulers and the ruled. The amount of information required to solve such a problem and the means to solve it are provided by the development of electronic computers of great sophistication. The complexity of this way of life is so great that computers will necessarily be the main tools for guiding individual and institutional interaction.

The size, variation, and complexity of the institutions of atomic society are greater than those of any previously described way of life. When the world is completely made over, and worldwide controls are necessary for such things as management of the climate, it becomes essential that the entire social structure—religious, military, economic, and political—be under centralized control. The entire population of the earth must become one unit under centralized control, for every part of the system must be carefully coordinated if it is to remain efficiently balanced. This implies most generally that one political institution must control all the nations of the earth. The atomic way of life cannot be successful with less than the cooperation of all nations united. Such unification is most likely to occur first not through universal agreement, but through conquest by the nation or nations whose leaders make the most effective use of atomic weapons as instruments of coercion and diplomacy. This does not preclude the very limited use of such weapons in warfare for these purposes, but as we have already remarked, extensive atomic warfare is apt to lead to the destruction of civilization if not the extinction of man.

If man cannot find a way of regulating his numbers at a level that can be supported by a man-made, man-controlled, worldwide, balanced, ecological system, then it is possible that social discontent will be so great that atomic war will break out. The possible extermination of the human species could follow if, after having found brilliant solutions to the problems of protection and nutrition, man cannot also solve the problems of reproduction.

III | APPLICA-TIONS AND EVALUA-TIONS

Ii

11 | THE USE OF MODELS IN ANTHROPOLOGY

The descriptions in Chapters 3–10 are outlines of hypothetical models of possible ways of life. The models themselves are conceived through the processes of abstraction from and logical analysis of the pertinent factual data. Each model represents only what we consider to be essential elements and relations of the way of life under discussion. These models are not described with the thought that they might actually be constructed but, like all anthropological models, are offered for the purposes of understanding, to help make possible the scientific explanation and prediction of man's behavior and of his culture.

The conceptual construction of anthropological models is by no means uncommon. Every description given by any anthropologist of any human society or cultural object is a model in the sense defined above. This is no radical thesis. Anyone who describes anything must choose or abstract from among its myriad characteristics, aspects, and relations a limited number of these to refer to in his description. What the description literally describes is an abstraction from the object. Thus, any object is described by referring to a selection of its features. The actual object is more complex than what is literally described but nevertheless is an exemplification of the type, or model, presented by the description. Since in describing an object a person must choose, or abstract, characteristics to mention, we can conclude that an anthropologist describes the objects of his investigations from a certain viewpoint, which leads him to stress some elements and relations and to ignore others. What he describes is really his picture of reality, which may be quite different from the picture seen and described by an anthropologist of different methodological or ideological persuasion. It is the point embodied in Protagoras' statement that "man is the measure of all things" and quite effectively illustrated for contemporary anthropologists in Sherwood L. Washburn's lecture entitled "An Ape's Eye-View of Human Evolution." [1] Anthropological models are high-level classifications resulting from the extension of the process of categorization, which is presented in Chapter 1 as the essential foundation of all human knowledge. Even the most elaborate conceptual model does not constitute *scientific* knowledge, however, unless it is presented in the form of, or is a part of, a lawlike generalization. And only then can such models be said to be scientifically true or false to reality.

Anthropologists sometimes give descriptions of cultural entities that refer to elements that are not present in reality. These models are not necessarily false, however. Every model that represents an abstraction of selected elements from factual data is in a strict sense true to the data, and every model that does not embody a contradiction is acceptable simply as a model. The criterion usually applied in rejecting some of these models as "false" and accepting others as "true" to reality is one of utility. If the model is useful for scientific explanation or prediction, it is said to be a true picture of reality; if it is not useful for scientific explanation or prediction, it is said to

---

[1] In Paul L. DeVore, ed., *The Origin of Man* (New York: Wenner-Gren Foundation for Anthropological Research, 1965), pp. 38–96.

falsify reality. Therefore, anthropologists test the aspects stressed by a model for their utility in scientific explanation and prediction.

It is important to recognize that any anthropological description defines a model and that any such model can be tested for "truth" (scientific relevance) by organizing its description in the form of one or more lawlike generalizations and then checking to see if it is useful for explaining or predicting in the area under consideration. Of course, descriptions can be abstracted from the factual data that are not useful for scientific explanation and prediction but are, for example, for aesthetic appreciation. And it would be naive to think that it is usually a simple matter to arrange descriptions in the form of lawlike generalizations that may or may not be scientifically useful. Below we discuss the value of some descriptions that are acceptable as historical narratives, even though they do not provide good grounds for explanation and prediction, and examine the difficulties of giving descriptions of models in terms of lawlike generalizations.

Scientific laws and theories, as defined in Chapter 1, can be seen as models of different levels of complexity, described in terms of lawlike generalizations and axiomatic systems. In these terms one can say that it is the business of the scientist first to build models of the reality he experiences, i.e., to categorize or classify the elements of his subject matter. Then he must reformulate his descriptions of these conceptualizations in terms of lawlike generalizations. Finally, he must attempt to organize the generalizations into an axiomatized system, or theory.

Let us now consider the nature and function of the models of ways of life described in Chapters 3–10. Although each description contains statements in the form of lawlike generalizations (for example, an animal must satisfy his requirements for protection, nutrition, and reproduction), none of the eight descriptions is explicitly expressed in the form of a compound lawlike generalization, nor are the sets of lawlike generalizations in any of the descriptions explicitly axiomatized in the form of a scientific theory. Each of the eight descriptions can be taken as a model—a categorization—of a way of life. As a classificatory model, then, each of these models is true to factual data merely by virtue of having been abstracted from it. However, as is quite apparent, each model is described in a series of statements that are explicitly or implicitly lawlike generalizations. They could be linked together randomly as one compound lawlike generalization. They are, in fact, given in each chapter in an order that suggests a quasi-axiomatization. By adhering strictly to the statement form of lawlike generalization, one could present each of these eight models in the form of a scientific theory. Each model, then, is useful in the pursuit of knowledge because it is an obvious categorization of actual ways of life, and each model is useful in the pursuit of scientific knowledge because it can be described in terms of lawlike generalizations that can be axiomatized as a theory.

Suppose we take the model of Chapter 3 as a generalized theory about nonhuman primate ways of life. To test its scientific utility, one must first reexamine the factual material about the different species of nonhuman primates from which the generalized description is abstracted to be certain that in its axiomatized form the description does not give a distorted picture. It is not surprising that the unaxiomatized model is true to the facts, since it is abstracted directly from them. But when the model is reformulated in terms of axiomatized, lawlike generalizations, some of its several possible axiomatizations may not accurately reflect the factual data. According to principles of formal logic too specialized to be given here, it is not necessarily true that what can be deduced from one axiomatization of a set of generalizations is the same as what can be deduced from another axiomatization of the same set. Once an axiomatization is found that "fits" the data, then one might test it further by deducing a new theorem from it, expressing this theorem in the form of a lawlike generalization, and checking it in the field to see if it is exemplified by the behavior of the various species of nonhuman primates under investigation. The general model in Chapter 3 is abstracted from the specific models of several species of nonhuman primates described by a number of different field ethologists. We could obtain preliminary confirmation of a new theorem deduced from the general axiomatization by finding that it is exemplified by theorems deducible from axiomatizations of each specific model. But the final test must come from empirical observation in the field: the new general theorem is held to be true to reality, i.e., useful for scientific explanation and prediction, only if it is found to be exemplified in the actual behavior of primates of the various species under the general theory's comprehension. If the general theory is confirmed by these tests, then it can be used as a scientific explanation of the behavior of the individual animals and species within its domain. Although, as we said above, the unaxiomatized general description itself is obviously true to the facts to the extent that it is a direct abstraction from them, an axiomatization is not necessarily true to reality, but must be tested empirically before it can be accepted. Consequently, there is no circularity involved in explaining behavior with the axiomatized form of a general description abstracted from that behavior.

An established theory can be used not only to explain behavior, but also to predict it. If one should discover a new species of nonhuman primate that on preliminary examination exemplified the major axioms (basic lawlike generalizations) of the theory, then one could predict that the way of life of this species would also exemplify theorems (other lawlike generalizations) deducible from these axioms. The ideal model, then, is scientifically useful for both explanation and prediction. If the predictions are not borne out, one may find either that the new species is not of the same type as those comprehended under the theory or that some fault in the theory requires its reformulation so that it does explain and predict the behavior of the new species.

In the sequence of the eight models we have described, basic principles discussed in detail in early chapters carry over and are applicable in later chapters where they may be merely mentioned. Because the basic axioms—laws—of each successive model are cumulative from the preceding models, all eight descriptions can be connected. An examination of all eight models together makes possible higher levels of lawlike generalization, which can stand as axioms of a grand theory. For example, given an increase in total energy consumption by a given number of individuals, population will increase. Or, given an increase in population, the variety and complexity of social institutions will increase. Here again, the test of these lawlike generalizations and of the theory constructed from their axiomatization must be laboratory or field examination of the factual data from which the original descriptions are abstracted.

Each of the models in Chapters 3–10 is described insofar as possible in an isolated, atemporal context, and our discussion of models in this chapter also largely avoids consideration of the empirical fact that things change through time. However, these models do have application to the scientific understanding of change in a temporal context: evolutionary change and historical change. We shall see that in the study of evolution and in the study of history, it is necessary to consider both particular and general change.

The general biological theory of evolution embodies the basic principle that change of species is in the direction of increased adaptation to given environments; this adaptation is expressed in terms of the successively more complex and varied structure, function, and behavior of the individual organisms that make up the species. Single organisms do not undergo evolutionary change, but the species to which they belong evolve through time as a result of the survival and reproduction of individuals whose genes—through fortunate combinations or minor but progressive mutations—give rise to individuals that are successively better adapted to the environment. A particular line of organisms confined to a specific environment may evolve phylogenetically through several species, each of which is more specialized than the last in its adaptation to the environment. The result may be a species so specialized that an environmental change, a sudden change in climate, for example, could cause its extinction because it could not adapt rapidly enough, if at all, to the new environmental conditions. A particular line of organisms that exists in an area in which there is a wide variety of environments or that ranges over a variety of environments may evolve phylogenetically through several species, each of which is more generalized than the last in its adaptation to the variety of environments. The result may be a species so generalized that only the most radical environmental change could endanger its survival.

In studying the particular course of evolution of a specific species, as in the two examples given above, a person investigates the actual phylogenetic line of species preceding it. On the level of individual organisms, the investigation proceeds along the ancestral line. In studying the general course of evolution of the most specialized species adapted to a specific environment or of the most generalized species adapted to the widest range of environments, he investigates the line of species in a hierarchy determined by degree of adaptation to the specific environment or range of environments. Those species that have individuals least adapted to the environment in terms of their structure, function, and behavior are at the bottom of the hierarchy, with increasingly specialized individuals at higher and higher levels. In the investigation of general evolution, all species are ranked without the requirement that the hierarchical line be phylogenetic or ancestral.

Both particular and general courses of evolution can lead, as we have seen, either to highly specialized or to highly generalized species. If the varied environments of the earth as a whole are considered as one combined environment, one to which a species can or must adapt, then we can say that the species most specialized in adaptation to this complex environment is the species that because of the structure, function, and behavior of its individual members is most generalized. In discussions of particular and general evolution it is sometimes erroneously stated that particular (phylogenetic) evolution leads to species specialization, whereas general (not necessarily phylogenetic) evolution leads to species generalization. Actually, any species can be considered the result of both particular evolution, along its own phylogenetic line, and general evolution, across phylogenetic lines. Particular and general evolution, for example, resulted in man, a generalized species that is, because of its very generalization, highly specialized for adaptation to the complex environment of the earth as a whole.

The theory of evolution provides scientific understanding of man and his culture, as well as of man and nature. We could avoid arguments about the legitimacy of utilizing the biological theory of evolution to explain the result of human behavior—some consider culture to be superorganic—by merely generalizing the theory of evolution: change in time is in the direction of successively more complex and varied structure, function, and behavior of the individual entities that belong to the classes under consideration. If we accept an interpretation of the second law of thermodynamics—which implies that the total movement of the universe is in the direction of homogeneity, not complexity—then the general theory of evolution is not true for the universe as a whole; but the general theory of evolution does seem to apply to living organisms and to man's cultural behavior and institutions. We do not, however, wish to avoid arguments about the legitimacy of utilizing the biological theory of evolution to explain the results of human behavior. It is our thesis that man is a part of nature—an organic part—and that it is appropriate to describe his behavior in biological terms. We do not mean to say that there are no specifically psychological, anthropological, sociological, and culturological methods, vocabularies, and laws. What we do mean to insist is that because the objects of study in psychology, anthropology, sociology, and culturology derive from the organic bodies, human minds, and intelligent behavior of men, a legitimate description of these objects can be given in biological terms. Because of his biological nature, the scientific understanding of man must be grounded in biological terms. Biological organisms—at least as species if not as individuals, and at least over fairly long periods of time—do not proceed toward entropy (a dissipation of energy) but toward more and more increased concentrations of energy flow. This movement is exhibited in the activity of all organisms and in particular in the activities of man. If we admit for the moment that man's cultural objects, behavior, and institutions have changed progressively in the direction of more complexity and (perhaps because of) more concentration of energy flow, then we can explain this fact by accepting human culture in general biological terms as the adaptive behavior (or results of the adaptive behavior) of a certain species: *Homo sapiens.* This is to say that the theory of evolution is applicable to species of biological organisms and to their structure, function, and behavior. Man is one such species. If the theory of evolution validly provides scientific understanding of the structure, function, and behavior of other organisms, it is probable that it will also provide scientific understanding of man.

The claim has been made that just as the biological is a level above the inorganic and the biological universe therefore requires principles of understanding (such as the theory of evolution) different from the principles required for the understanding of the inorganic universe (such as the second law of thermodynamics), so the cultural is a level above the biological and thus requires different principles of understanding. This superorganic level is said to be nonbiological—rooted in neither physical nor biological laws. However, we do not find that the so-called superorganic lends itself to scientific investigation as do both the inorganic and the biological levels. Public methods of observing and describing the superorganic have not been described, nor have public methods for testing lawlike generalizations and theories about the superorganic been devised. It is quite possible that the superorganic is simply the supernatural (a name that has gone out of style) and that some of those investigators who are most concerned with exhibiting the mysteries of the superorganic are not primarily concerned with science but are worried about theological problems of free will and the afterlife. We do not mean to belittle these concerns. We wish to argue only that most discussions of the superorganic have not been scientifically fruitful; that is, the superorganic, as above or separate from physical and biological theory, has not been demonstrated to be a domain that can be studied with the general scientific method as can the inorganic and the biological. Notable examples of how culture *can* be studied scientifically as a domain above the biological are found in the works of Leslie A. White and of Julian R. Steward, for whom culture may be superorganic but *not* in any sense supernatural. Since our concern is with the scientific understanding of man as a part of nature, let us consider whether an understanding of man's culture can be obtained by subsuming it under the general theory of biological evolution.

We have organized the descriptions of models of ways of life in a sequence proceeding from simple to complex structures, functions, and behavior, from less to more utilization and concentration of energy flow for a given population, and from homogeneous and simple to heterogeneous and complex social institutions. It is obvious that this sequence can be viewed as a model of both particular and general cultural evolution. It is not a model of the evolution of culture in general, since we have concentrated on those aspects of culture that can be readily linked to man's direct interactions with the physical environment. It can be taken, however, as a fairly complete model of the evolution of man's material culture and of some aspects of the more important social institutions directly related to material culture. Is it a scientifically useful model?

With respect to particular evolution, the validity of the model is hypothetical. It cannot be tested at the present time because we know of no group of human beings with an endogamous ancestry and a culture that has changed over this time span without interference. Man's ability to communicate knowledge makes the diffusion and assimilation of elements from the culture of one group into another very nearly unavoidable on earth.

The fact that cultural diffusion does take place, that human groups influence one another, and particularly the fact that groups with less complex cultures are modified by contact with groups having more complex cultures makes the model of general evolution pertinent and testable when applied to the development of human culture as a whole. Diffusion, or cultural borrowing, provides a means for explaining why the course of general cultural evolution is not necessarily phylogenetic but can progress from one cultural group to another, even when the two groups have no ancestral line in common. The model can be taken, then, as a hypothetical representation of the theory of general evolution. It is scientifically useful because when the factual data of anthropology are examined, the theory is seen to provide grounds for the explanation and the prediction of cultural elements, as well as for the progressive development of culture from simple to complex forms. When the sequence of eight models of ways of life is taken as the basis of a theory of general cultural evolution, then the theory is empirically testable. The theory is derived, therefore, from experience and tested by experience. Examination of the factual data shows that culture has indeed changed through time from simple to complex and that this progression has spread by diffusion. The theory provides an explanation for the general development of culture and for the fact that in some parts of the world a group of men may live an industrial way of life even though their fathers lived a hunting-and-gathering way of life. It also allows one to predict, for example, some of the general cultural changes that are likely to result if a group of village farmers discover oil underlying the fields they own. Human culture does seem to evolve along the lines and in the way the theory of general evolution suggests.

We do not claim that the model of sequential development based on the descriptions of ways of life in Chapters 3–10 is complete. As a hypothetical device derived from factual data, it can always be improved as more factual data are accumulated. But we do claim that it is part of the scientist's task to frame such models—to categorize —and that such models are necessary to the development of scientific theories. The model in this book can be used, as we have shown, to develop and test theories of cultural evolution. We would further claim that the scientific value of the theory of cultural evolution has been adequately demonstrated. The model allows for a quasi-axiomatization of lawlike generalizations to form theories that can predict and explain human behavior.

We now turn to the question of whether models are useful in the study of history—and, by extension, in the "historical" sciences, such as anthropology, geology, paleontology. The historian's task is said by some to be nothing more than recording events. It does not matter what events occur or in what order they occur, for the essential characteristic that makes an event amenable to historical treatment is the temporal form—the fact that the events change through time. It is often claimed that history as narrative is nontheoretical, that it cannot be predicted or explained, and that no laws can be derived from it. However, since it is practically impossible for all aspects of all events to be recorded, a historian must select which events and which aspects of these events he will describe. In effect, any historical narrative is descriptive of a model in the sense defined above. Thus, there can be scientific history as well as narrative history. The principles of selection can be such that the model itself suggests lawlike generalizations that lend themselves to axiomatization. Making a descriptive, in this case narrative, model is the first step toward formulating a scientific theory. Various historical narratives suggest cyclical, religious, economic, great-man, and *Zeitgeist* theories of history. Obviously, the theory of evolution sketched above can be viewed as an evolutionary theory of history. The evolutionary theory of history is certainly viable—if we consider the effect of cultural diffusion—although other theories of history may be useful as well.

It is worthwhile to examine the reasons and confusions which have led some people to say that there can be no science of history, that the methodology of history must be different in kind from the methodology of the physical and biological sciences, and thus that the search for laws of history is futile because there are no laws of history. It is important to understand the genesis of these disclaimers because they are often made about anthropology. We defend the thesis that history and anthropology are not just narrative chronicles, but sciences that are methodologically and logically similar to the physical and biological sciences.

Scientific explanation and prediction depend, as we said in Chapter 1, on the subsumption of particular events under lawlike generalizations. With a lawlike generalization one can explain what has happened or predict what will happen when an ounce of sulfur is burned in air; in general terms, one can describe what happens to a given type of object in a given type of circumstances. The concern of physical scientists is with the derivation of lawlike generalizations from experimental observation of particular objects of the same type. When a physical scientist feels that he has collected sufficient data from his particular observations, then he can generalize from this data, formulating a law that may or may not be confirmed by further observation and experiment. It may be that physical scientists are most concerned with formulating general laws. However, the laws they do formulate are, if confirmed, useful for the scientific explanation and prediction of aspects of particular events.

What is important to recognize here is the relation between the particular and the general. Particular events provide the bases for, and are explained and predicted by reference to, lawlike generalizations. A lawlike generalization derived from observation of and experimentation on particular pieces of sulfur can be seen as a description of a type of chemical event. This type—or model, in our terminology—is not an actual but a conceptual abstraction. When scientists talk of *the* chemical reaction, they have in mind a type or model reaction. They sometimes say that the chemical reaction is repeatable, but since it is just a hypothetical model it is neither repeatable nor nonrepeatable. To say that the chemical reaction is repeatable is to say that *a* chemical reaction of this same type can be produced using a particular, actual example of the type of chemical element described in the generalization under the particular, actual circumstances described in the generalization.

Students of history, anthropology, and the other "historical" sciences, such as geology and paleontology, are popularly thought to be concerned primarily (and some, exclusively) with particular events. But this would confine them to the task of writing narrative chronicles, and few historians have ever limited themselves strictly to recording events. The best writing of history is narrative that also provides explanations. Such explanations are made with reference to lawlike generalizations. The laws appealed to in many cases are from the physical and biological sciences as well as from psychology and other social sciences. But is there any reason why there cannot be lawlike generalizations derived explicitly from the narrative data of history? Why do some historians claim there can be no laws of history? The reason is that they are primarily interested in particular events and are so impressed with their particularity that they may feel each event is so different from every other that it is futile even to classify it, let alone to try to derive lawlike generalizations. History, they say, does not repeat itself, but neither does any particular event studied in the physical sciences; no particular event is repeatable as such. However, different physical events of the same type occur more frequently in temporal sequence, so that it is often incorrectly said that chemical reactions are repeatable, which means only that different particular reactions of the same general type can occur.

What the narrative historian might be claiming by saying that there are no repeatable events and thus no laws in history is that one cannot formulate types, or models, of historical events. As we have seen, since classification depends on principles of selection, *any* classificatory scheme provides the necessary grounds for lawlike generalizations and scientific theories. If each event studied by historians is so different that it is impossible to categorize events according to types, then obviously no scientific laws or theories can be derived for these events. However, it is obvious that historians do categorize their objects of study in their treatment of periods, power, politics, and so on. Different historical events of the same type do occur in temporal sequence. Is the narrative historian claiming, therefore, that such categorizations do not lend themselves to reformulation as lawlike generalizations?

There is no logical reason why it should be impossible to categorize, generalize, and theorize about the events of history: it is, in fact, done by historians all the time. Consequently, what the narrative historians must be claiming is that in fact these laws and theories, although they may exist, are not confirmable or that, if they can be confirmed, they are trivial or useless. However, historians constantly employ these "useless" lawlike generalizations and theories to make understandable to their readers the particular events they describe. Thus, history does not differ logically from physics. Why, then, are historical laws often called trivial or useless? In what ways *do* history, anthropology, and the other "historical" sciences differ from such sciences as physics?

The subject matter of history—indeed, of all the "historical" sciences—is made scientifically understandable by the subsumption of particular events under lawlike generalizations and theories. However, unlike the subject matter of physics or chemistry, for example, the events studied in history are often so extensive in space and time that it is difficult for men to observe them adequately or to manipulate or duplicate them in experiment. They are sometimes so rare that only one occurrence of each is known. And they are usually so complex that human intelligence is not adequate to comprehend the complexity or to factor out the essential elements of the situation. In contrast, the events and objects that are the subject matter of chemistry are often restricted in space and time so that it is easy for man to observe them adequately and to manipulate or duplicate them in experiment. They are usually fairly common in our world, and their complexity is often of the degree that man can comprehend and describe in terms of scientific law and theory. These empirical circumstances of size, occurrence, complexity, and of human observational, manipulative, and intellectual capacities are the reasons the sciences of physics and chemistry have progressed more (have more confirmable scientific laws and theories) than the sciences of history and anthropology. And because of these same circumstances, the laws of physics and chemistry are more useful (more readily applicable to their subject matter) than the laws of history and anthropology. There is nothing intrinsic in the subject matter of history and anthropology that makes it less susceptible to scientific treatment than the subject matter of physics and chemistry. It is simply that the spatial and temporal extension, rarity of occurrence, and great complexity of the objects of history and anthropology are such that human beings cannot easily derive laws from them.

The historical laws that can be derived—for example, in given circumstances, an increase in population will lead to an increase in complexity of social organization—are often so general that they are not as useful for explaining and predicting particular events as historians would like them to be. This is not to say that they do not explain and predict in a general way. Such broad, lawlike generalizations as these historical laws provide the background for all our understanding of historical events, but it is because of their great generality that they are sometimes called trivial or useless. Thus, most narrative historians probably do not really mean what they say—that there are no laws of history and that it is a mistake to look for them; they mean only that the laws that do exist and that we can derive are so general and often so obvious—and the understanding they provide is so general—that it is not worthwhile to spend much time looking for them.

On the other hand, extremely specific laws of history can also be derived. We may be interested in a particular event to such an extent that we specify the type or describe the model of that particular event so explicitly—including space and time coordinates—that logically there can be only one example of it. A reformulation of the description of the model in terms of a lawlike generalization would result in a confirmable law explaining the event, which, if it had been known prior to the event, could have been used to predict it. Since human intelligence seems to be limited so that such specific laws are never derived until after the event, however, they are not useful for prediction. Since, in addition, they are so specific that they explain only one event, and they appear to explain that one event merely with a description of everything known about the event reformulated as a lawlike generalization, they are often said not to be useful for explanation either. Once one knows what has happened, it is not very illuminating to delineate all the known circumstances and elements of the event and then to claim that in all similar circumstances where similar elements are involved, a similar event would occur if, given the particular space and time coordinates, there could logically be only one event of the type encompassed by the law.

The evaluations of the usefulness of the known laws of history in the last two paragraphs are, of course, fair enough. However, the usefulness of broad generalizations is in fact immense, and all historians admit this in practice, if not in theory. History could not be written without reference to them. They are also valuable for understanding which aspects of a situation are primary and which are secondary.

The historian wants laws that, like those of physics, are not so general as to be too broadly applicable and not so specific as to be too narrowly applicable. If man's observational or manipulative abilities were greater, or his lifespan longer, or his intellectual capacities greater, he might be able to derive these laws. Or if similar historical events occurred as frequently as, for example, ounces of sulfur, and we were as capable of studying them as we are of studying ounces of sulfur, then, too, we might be able to derive laws of history. However, given our limited capacities and the singularity and complexity of the historical events we study, there is only one way we can proceed in attempting to develop laws of history that provide useful scientific understanding by being neither too broad nor too narrow. We must construct hypothetical models based on synthesis from and logical analysis of the factual data at our disposal.

We have stressed that historical theories derived from such models may be very difficult to test given the rarity of historical events and our limited access to those that do occur. In particular, one can almost never actually experiment with this material. However, theories of history can be tested at least for feasibility by imagining various circumstances and then applying the theory to predict what would happen to given historical objects in such circumstances. Such procedures are called thought experiments. A theory tested in thought will be found acceptable if its explanatory and predictive power in imagined circumstances appears to be compatible with the rest of the historian's general knowledge about the subject matter. Since what will appear acceptable to one historian may not appear acceptable to another and since there is no practical way to test the theories in actual experience, such a method of confirming theories with thought experiments is weak. Thus there will probably always be competing theories in history, just as there are, but in a much more testable arena, competing theories in physics. That theories in history are more tenuous than those in physics does not mean, however, that they are not of the same logical form, nor does it mean that they are not scientifically useful. What has been said here of history can also be said in large part of anthropology, although anthropologists can test their theories in the field more readily than historians can. It is the anthropologist's task as a scientist continually to refine the models based upon the continually accumulating factual data, for it is only with reference to these models that scientific understanding can be attained.

12 | HUMAN ECOLOGY

We have called this work an anthropological essay in human ecology because we believe the basic relation between man and nature is ecological. As June Helm concludes in "The Ecological Approach in Anthropology," man is necessarily a part of an ecological community, and no matter how complicated and removed many of his activities are from direct contact and contention with the physical environment, man remains a part of nature.[1] This conclusion is concisely expressed by Robert J. Braidwood in his article "Prelude to Civilization":

> Given the biological nature of man, the [direct man-nature] relationship must obviously continue to exist, and its balance, however subtle, must be maintained if the species is to survive.[2]

We believe that our study is a step toward the confirmation of a theory based on this viewpoint. We have constructed one of the

---

[1] *The American Journal of Sociology*, Vol. 67 (1962), pp. 630–39.
[2] Carl H. Kraeling and Robert McC. Adams, eds., *City Invincible: A Symposium on Urbanization and Cultural Development in the Ancient Near East* (Chicago: University of Chicago Press, 1960), p. 311.

possible "imaginative models as a framework against which to set problem-oriented field research," [3] and of course it is with the progression of knowledge derived from field work that the model will be refined and eventually confirmed or rejected.

The model we have built and the laws we have derived lead to conclusions that parallel, in a smaller scope, many of those found in Leslie A. White's monumental work, *The Evolution of Culture*. The major law deriving from White's investigations is as follows:

> *Culture advances as the amount of energy harnessed per capita per year increases, or as the efficiency or economy of the means of controlling energy is increased, or both.* [4]

This lawlike generalization is certainly one of the most important for the scientific understanding of man, and it is one that we have derived for our model. It helps to support our belief that the best interpretation of our model is as an evolutionary theory. This is not the place to defend White against his critics, but we do believe that many of the criticisms of White will be seen as misguided if his work is taken to be scientific in the sense defined in Chapter 11. It is essential to overcome the strictures against scientific work that, as Marshall D. Sahlins points out in "Evolution: Specific and General," have stemmed from the fact that "the search for broad generalization . . . has been virtually declared unscientific (!) by twentieth-century, academic, particularistic American anthropology." [5] There is, in fact, no better defense of and exemplification of anthropology as a science than in Sahlins and Service's book.

It is doubtful that anyone today will argue against the value of

---

[3] *Ibid.*, p. 310.
[4] *The Evolution of Culture: The Development of Civilization to the Fall of Rome* (New York: McGraw-Hill, 1959), p. 56. The italics are White's.
[5] Marshall D. Sahlins and Elman R. Service, eds., *Evolution and Culture* (Ann Arbor: University of Michigan Press, 1960), p. 29. The exclamation point is Sahlins'.

models for scientific understanding as we have presented the case for them. Just as there are presuppositions in metaphysics, so there are presuppositions in anthropology, and even the least culture-bound worker will be paralyzed in the field if he does not have some notion of the sort of data he wishes to collect. Any categorization leads to model making, and without categories and models, there are no data on which to build scientific understanding and knowledge. Careful categorization and model building is exemplified in Julian R. Steward's important work, *Theory of Culture Change*, and advocated by Walter Goldschmidt in *Man's Way* and in *Comparative Functionalism*.

Perhaps the most strident objection to the approach used in the present study will come from those who are haunted by the specter of environmental determinism. Does the ecological approach commit one to a view of environmental determinism? In a sense it does, but then scientific knowledge of any sort is deterministic. Science rests on the principles that there is no effect without a cause and that from similar causes similar effects result. The search in science is for universal [6] laws. When we discover that something we thought was subsumable under a universal law does not in fact behave as the law predicts, then we do not—as scientists—argue that the universe is not lawful. Instead, we look for an explanation of the deviant behavior in terms of other universal laws. Although the attainment of omniscience is physically and intellectually impossible for man, the ideal of scientific research is to find universal laws with which we can explain and predict the behavior of everything. To say that we live in a universe that can be understood rationally is to say that everything in the universe can be described in terms of lawlike generalizations. This faith is sometimes expressed in terms of the principle of uniformitarianism, which, in its most fundamental sense, says that under similar circumstances, similar objects will behave in simi-

---

[6] See Chapter 1, note 1.

lar ways. We construct our models of ways of life on this principle. They reflect our view that in similar situations, similar problems will have similar solutions.

Some people reject the idea that there can be laws for human behavior by saying the human will is free. This statement, which suggests a retreat to magic and mysticism, can be interpreted in only one way that is consistent with scientific investigation: although there certainly are natural causes of human behavior, such as those expressed in the many lawlike generalizations of the social sciences, many of these causes and their effects are so subtle and complex that human beings have not yet understood them or are not capable of understanding them. The uncertainty in human life would come, then, not from any free, or uncaused, behavior, but from our ignorance of many of the important laws of human behavior. This position is not inconsistent with the belief that human beings can, by considered choice, determine their own behavior under some circumstances. But to claim that there are no uniform causes of human behavior and that there are no uniformities of human behavior (above a certain level) that can be described in terms of lawlike generalizations is to deny that man is a part of nature. If man is not a part of nature, he cannot be understood scientifically. We believe the facts show that man *is* a part of nature, that there are laws which describe the determination of all his behavior, and thus that there is a science of anthropology.

We do not claim that the physical environment directly determines all man's behavior, but it must all be related to the physical environment in some way. In our model we have shown the lines of influence that radiate through all man's activities from his primary need to cope with the physical environment. It is the physical environment that sets the possibilities for and the limitations of cultural development. Nature poses the problems for man, who is an animal that must live on the earth. He must sustain himself with resources of the earth, and it is only within the range of potentialities presented by these resources that man can develop his culture.

If the environment were too hostile, man would not survive; and it is certain that man puts his species in danger of extinction if he reproduces in numbers far beyond the potentiality of the earth to support. These remarks appear so obvious as to be tautological. They are, in fact, conclusions based on considering man as a part of the earth's total ecological community.

Besides determining the grand possibilities and the ultimate limits of human cultural development, the physical environment also determines the behavior of man and the structure and functions of his social institutions in myriad lesser ways. What foods man eats, what climates he lives in, what work he does, and what medicines he takes all involve the effect of physical environment in direct and significant ways on his physical and mental behavior and thus on the social institutions in which he interacts with nature in the broad sense, including other men. Most of these effects are common knowledge, so much so that many of the truths of anthropogeography, human geography, and now human ecology are denigrated not because they are false, but because they seem to be organized to tell us what we already know, or because they do not tell us what we want to know in enough detail. As we have said, the difficulty in formulating exceptionless lawlike generalizations about the relations between the physical environment and man does not stem from the lack of uniformities so much as from man's inability to comprehend the many factors involved. If we are to have a scientific understanding of man, however, we must continue to seek these uniformities and to attempt to formulate lawlike generalizations about them.

Finally, we are not convinced that the lawlike generalizations of the social sciences are generally such common knowledge as some would have us believe. Our basic conclusion—man is part of the ecological community of the earth and can survive as a species only if he does not disrupt the ecological balance of the earth—seems to be ignored or denied by many of the most powerful men on earth today. Masses of men on earth are unaware of this law or disregard it; they continue to reproduce excessively in the face of famine. To keep in ecological balance with nature does not mean that man should go "back to nature." On the contrary, if man is willing to accept the population level the earth's finite resources will support, he is capable of remaking the physical environment and rebalancing the ecology of the earth to meet his own needs. Man has the technical knowledge to do this now. Knowledge derived in part from the science of anthropology shows that it must be done. Ecological balance is essential to human protection, nutrition, and reproduction and is therefore the ultimate relationship man must maintain with nature.

SELECTED
BIBLIOGRAPHY

Adams, Robert McC. *The Evolution of Urban Society: Early Meso-potamia and Prehispanic Mexico*. Chicago: Aldine, 1966.

———. "The Origin of Cities." *Scientific American*, Vol. 203 (1960), pp. 153–68.

———. "The Evolutionary Process in Early Civilizations," in Sol Tax, ed., *Evolution After Darwin*, Vol. 2, *The Evolution of Man: Man, Culture, and Society*. Chicago: University of Chicago Press, 1960, pp. 153–68.

Barth, Frederik. "Ecologic Relationships of Ethnic Groups in Swat, North Pakistan." *American Anthropologist*, Vol. 57 (1956), pp. 1079–89.

———. *Models of Social Organization*. London: Royal Anthropological Institute of Great Britain and Ireland (Occasional Paper Number 23), 1966.

———. *Nomads of South Persia: The Basseri Tribe of the Khamseh Confederacy*. Oslo: Oslo University Press, 1961.

———. *Political Leadership Among Swat Pathans*. (London School of Economics Monographs on Social Anthropology Number 19) London: Athlone Press, 1959.

Bartholomew, George A., Jr., and Birdsell, Joseph B. "Ecology and the Protohominids." *American Anthropologist,* Vol. 55 (1953), pp. 481–98.

Bates, Marston. *Man in Nature,* 2nd ed. Englewood Cliffs, N.J.: Prentice-Hall, 1964.

Bennett, John W. "Further Remarks on Foster's 'Image of Limited Good.'" *American Anthropologist,* Vol. 68 (1966), pp. 206–10.

Bergmann, Gustav. *Philosophy of Science.* Madison: University of Wisconsin Press, 1957.

Binford, Lewis R., and Binford, Sally R. "The Predatory Revolution: A Consideration of the Evidence for a New Subsistence Level." *American Anthropologist,* Vol. 68 (1966), pp. 508–12.

Brace, C. Loring. *The Stages of Human Evolution: Human and Cultural Origins.* Englewood Cliffs, N.J.: Prentice-Hall, 1967.

Braidwood, Robert J. "The Agricultural Revolution." *Scientific American,* Vol. 203 (1960), pp. 131–48.

———. "Levels in Prehistory: A Model for Consideration of Evidence," in Sol Tax, ed., *Evolution After Darwin,* Vol. 2, *The Evolution of Man: Man, Culture, and Society.* Chicago: University of Chicago Press, 1960, pp. 143–51.

———. *Prehistoric Men,* 7th ed. Glenview, Ill.: Scott, Foresman, 1967.

———. "Prelude to Civilization," in Carl H. Kraeling and Robert McC. Adams, eds., *City Invincible: A Symposium on Urbanization and Cultural Development in the Ancient Near East.* Chicago: University of Chicago Press, 1960, pp. 297–313.

———, and Willey, Gordon R., eds. *Courses Toward Urban Life: Archeological Considerations of Some Cultural Alternates.* Chicago: Aldine, 1962.

Braithwaite, Richard Bevan. *Scientific Explanation: A Study of the Function of Theory, Probability and Law in Science.* New York and London: Cambridge University Press, 1953.

Bresler, Jack B., ed. *Human Ecology: Selected Readings.* Reading, Pa.: Addison-Wesley, 1966.

Brown, Harrison. *The Challenge of Man's Future: An Inquiry Concerning the Condition of Man During the Years Ahead.* New York: Viking Press, 1954.

Bryan, Alan L. "The Essential Morphological Basis for Human Culture." *Current Anthropology,* Vol. 4 (1963), pp. 297–306.

Butterfield, Herbert. "The Scientific Revolution." *Scientific American,* Vol. 203 (1960), pp. 173–92.

Butzer, Karl W. *Environment and Archeology.* Chicago: Aldine, 1964.

Campbell, Bernard G. *Human Evolution: An Introduction to Man's Adaptations.* Chicago: Aldine, 1966.

Carpenter, C. R. *Naturalistic Behavior of Nonhuman Primates.* University Park: Pennsylvania State University Press, 1964.

———. "Territoriality: A Review of Concepts and Problems," in Anne Roe and George Gaylord Simpson, eds., *Behavior and Evolution.* New Haven: Yale University Press, 1958, pp. 224–50.

Childe, V. Gordon. *Man Makes Himself,* 3rd ed. New York: New American Library, 1951.

———. *The Prehistory of European Society.* Harmondsworth, Middlesex: Penguin Books, 1958.

———. *Social Evolution.* New York: Henry Schuman, 1951.

———. *What Happened in History.* Harmondsworth, Middlesex: Penguin Books, 1942.

Clark, Grahame. *From Savagery to Civilization.* New York: Schuman, 1953.

———. *The Stone Age Hunters.* London: Thames and Hudson, 1967.

———, and Piggott, Stuart. *Prehistoric Societies.* London: Hutchinson, 1965.

Clark, J. G. D. *Prehistoric Europe: The Economic Basis.* London: Methuen, 1952.

Cohen, Yehudi A., ed. *Man in Adaptation,* Vol. 1, *The Biosocial Background.* Chicago: Aldine, 1968.

————, ed. *Man in Adaptation*, Vol. 2, *The Cutural Present*. Chicago: Aldine, 1968.

Count, Earl W. "The Biological Basis of Human Sociality." *American Anthropologist*, Vol. 60 (1958), pp. 1049–85.

Deevey, Edward S., Jr. "The Human Population." *Scientific American*, Vol. 203 (1960), pp. 195–204.

Dethier, V. G., and Stellar, Eliot. *Animal Behavior: Its Evolutionary and Neurological Basis*, 2nd ed. Englewood Cliffs, N.J.: Prentice-Hall, 1964.

DeVore, Irven, ed. *Primate Behavior: Field Studies of Monkeys and Apes*. New York: Holt, Rinehart & Winston, 1965.

DeVore, Paul L., ed. *The Origin of Man*. New York: Wenner-Gren Foundation for Anthropological Research, 1965.

Dice, Lee R. *Man's Nature and Nature's Man: The Ecology of Human Communities*. Ann Arbor: University of Michigan Press, 1955.

Dobzhansky, Theodosius. "The Present Evolution of Man." *Scientific American*, Vol. 203 (1960), pp. 206–17.

Eimerl, Sarel, and DeVore, Irven. *The Primates*. New York: Time, 1965.

Flannery, Kent. "The Ecology of Early Food Production in Mesopotamia." *Science*, Vol. 147 (1965), pp. 1247–56.

Forde, C. Daryll. *Habitat, Economy and Society: A Geographical Introduction to Ethnology*. London: Methuen, 1934.

Foster, George M. "Foster's Reply to Kaplan, Saler, and Bennett." *American Anthropologist*, Vol. 68 (1966), pp. 210–14.

————. "Peasant Society and the Image of Limited Good." *American Anthropologist*, Vol. 67 (1965), pp. 293–315.

Freedman, Lawrence Zelic, and Roe, Anne. "Evolution and Human Behavior," in Anne Roe and George Gaylord Simpson, eds., *Behavior and Evolution*. New Haven: Yale University Press, 1958, pp. 455–79.

Freud, Sigmund. *Civilization and Its Discontents*, ed. and trans. by James Strachey. New York: Norton, 1962.

Gabel, Creighton, ed. *Man Before History*. Englewood Cliffs, N.J.: Prentice-Hall, 1964.

Gluckman, Max, and Eggan, Fred, eds. *The Relevance of Models for Social Anthropology* (Association of Social Anthropologists Monograph 1), London: Travistock, 1965.

Goldschmidt, Walter. *Comparative Functionalism: An Essay in Anthropological Theory*. Berkeley and Los Angeles: University of California Press, 1966.

———. *Man's Way: A Preface to the Understanding of Human Society*. New York: Holt, Rinehart & Winston, 1959.

Goodman, Nelson. *Fact, Fiction, and Forecast*, 2nd ed. New York: Bobbs-Merrill, 1965.

Hallowell, A. Irving. "Self, Society, and Culture in Phylogenetic Perspective," in Sol Tax, ed., *Evolution After Darwin*, Vol. 2, *The Evolution of Man, Culture and Society*. Chicago: University of Chicago Press, 1960, pp. 309–71.

Harlan, Jack R. "A Wild Wheat Harvest in Turkey." *Archaeology*, Vol. 20 (1967), pp. 197–201.

Helbaek, Hans. "How Farming Began." *Archaeology*, Vol. 12 (1959), pp. 183–89.

———. "Studying the Diet of Ancient Man." *Archaeology*, Vol. 14 (1961), pp. 95–101.

Helm, June. "The Ecological Approach in Anthropology." *The American Journal of Sociology*, Vol. 67 (1962), pp. 630–39.

Hempel, Carl G. *Aspects of Scientific Explanation, and other Essays in the Philosophy of Science*. New York: Free Press, 1965.

Hewes, Gordon W. "Food Transport and the Origin of Hominid Bipedalism." *American Anthropologist*, Vol. 63 (1961), pp. 687–710.

Hockett, Charles F. "Logical Considerations in the Study of Animal Communication," in W. E. Layon and W. N. Tavolga, eds., *Animal Sounds and Communication*. Washington, D. C.: American Institute of Biological Sciences, Publication No. 7, 1960, pp. 392–430.

————. "The Origin of Speech." *Scientific American*, Vol. 203 (1960), pp. 88–96.

————. "The Problem of Universals in Language," in Joseph H. Green, ed., *Universals of Language*. Cambridge, Mass.: Massachusetts Institute of Technology Press, 1963, pp. 1–22.

————, and Ascher, Robert. "The Human Revolution." *Current Anthropology*, Vol. 5 (1964), pp. 135–68.

Hole, Frank. "Investigating the Origins of Mesopotamian Civilization." *Science*, Vol. 153 (1966), pp. 605–11.

Homans, George C. *The Nature of Social Science*. New York: Harcourt, Brace & World, 1967.

Howell, F. Clark. *Early Man*. New York: Time, 1965.

Howells, William W. *Back of History: The Story of Our Origins*, 2nd ed. Garden City, N.Y.: Doubleday, 1963.

————. "The Distribution of Man." *Scientific American*, Vol. 203 (1960), pp. 113–27.

Huxley, Julian. "Man's Place and Role in Nature," in Lewis Leary, ed., *The Unity of Knowledge*. Garden City, N.Y.: Doubleday, 1955, pp. 79–97.

Imanishi, Kinji. "Social Organization of Subhuman Primates in their Natural Habitat." *Current Anthropology*, Vol. 1 (1960), pp. 393–407.

Kaplan, David. "The Superorganic: Science or Metaphysics?" *American Anthropologist*, Vol. 67 (1965), pp. 958–76.

————, and Saler, Benson. "Foster's 'Image of Limited Good': An Example of Anthropological Explanation." *American Anthropologist*, Vol. 68 (1966), pp. 202–06.

Kleindienst, Maxine R., and Watson, Patty Jo. " 'Action Archeology': The Archeological Inventory of a Living Community." *Anthropology Tomorrow*, Vol. 5 (1956), pp. 75–78.

Kortlandt, Adriaan. "Chimpanzees in the Wild." *Scientific American*, Vol. 206 (1962), pp. 128–34, 137–38.

Krader, Lawrence. *Formation of the State*. Englewood Cliffs, N.J.: Prentice-Hall, 1968.

Kraeling, Carl H., and Adams, Robert McC., eds. *City Invincible: A Symposium on Urbanization and Cultural Development in the Ancient Near East.* Chicago: University of Chicago Press, 1960.

Lancaster, Jane B. "On the Evolution of Tool-Using Behavior." *American Anthropologist,* Vol. 70 (1968), pp. 56–66.

Lawrence, Barbara. "Early Domestic Dogs." *Zeitschrift für Saugetierbunde,* Vol. 32 (1967), pp. 44–59.

Leakey, Louis S. B. "Facts Instead of Dogmas on Man's Origin," in Paul L. DeVore, ed., *The Origin of Man.* New York: Wenner-Gren Foundation for Anthropological Research, 1965, pp. 3–17.

Lebrun, J. "Natural Balances and Scientific Research." *Impact of Science on Society,* Vol. 14 (1964), pp. 19–37.

Lee, Richard B., and DeVore, Irven, eds. *Man the Hunter.* Chicago: Aldine, 1969.

Lenneberg, Eric H. *Biological Foundations of Language.* New York: Wiley, 1967.

———. "Language, Evolution, and Purposive Behavior," in Stanley Diamond, ed., *Culture in History: Essays in Honor of Paul Radin.* New York: Columbia University Press, 1960, pp. 869–93.

Marsh, George Perkins. *Man and Nature.* Cambridge: Belknap-Harvard, 1965. (Originally published in 1864.)

Meggars, Betty J. "Environmental Limitation on the Development of Culture." *American Anthropologist,* Vol. 56 (1954), pp. 801–23.

Morgan, Lewis Henry. *Ancient Society, or Researches in the Lines of Human Progress from Savagery, Through Barbarism to Civilization.* New York: Holt, 1877.

Morris, Charles. *Signs, Language, and Behavior.* Englewood Cliffs, N.J.: Prentice-Hall, 1946.

Oakley, Kenneth P. *Man the Tool-Maker,* 3rd ed., London: British Museum, 1956.

Odum, Eugene P. *Ecology.* New York: Holt, Rinehart & Winston, 1963.

Piggott, Stuart. *Ancient Europe from the Beginnings of Agriculture to Classical Antiquity: A Survey.* Chicago: Aldine, 1965.

Radin, Paul. *The World of Primitive Man.* New York: Schuman, 1953.

Redfield, Robert. *The Primitive World and Its Transformations.* Ithaca, N.Y.: Cornell University Press, 1953.

Reed, Charles A. "A Review of the Archeological Evidence on Animal Domestication in the Prehistoric Near East," in Robert J. Braidwood and Bruce Howe, eds., *Prehistoric Investigations in Iraqi Kurdistan.* Chicago: University of Chicago Press, 1960, pp. 119–45.

Reynolds, Peter Carlton. "Evolution of Primate Vocal-Auditory Communication Systems." *American Anthropologist,* Vol. 70 (1968), pp. 300–08.

Rudner, Richard S. *Philosophy of Social Science.* Englewood Cliffs, N.J.: Prentice-Hall, 1966.

Sahlins, Marshall D. "Evolution: Specific and General," in Marshall D. Sahlins and Elman R. Service, eds., *Evolution and Culture.* Ann Arbor: University of Michigan Press, 1960, pp. 12–44.

———. "The Origin of Society." *Scientific American,* Vol. 203 (1960), pp. 76–87.

———. *Tribesmen.* Englewood Cliffs, N.J.: Prentice-Hall, 1968.

———, and Service, Elman R., eds. *Evolution and Culture.* Ann Arbor: University of Michigan Press, 1960.

Schaller, George B. *The Mountain Gorilla: Ecology and Behavior.* Chicago: University of Chicago Press, 1963.

Schrier, A. M., Harlow, H. F., and Stollnitz, F., eds. 2 vols. *Behavior of Nonhuman Primates: Modern Research Trends.* New York: Academic, 1965.

Sears, Paul B. "Climate and Civilization," in Harlow Shapley, ed., *Climatic Change.* Cambridge, Mass.: Harvard University Press, 1953, pp. 35–50.

———. *The Ecology of Man.* Eugene: Oregon State System of Higher Education, 1957.

Service, Elman R. *The Hunters.* Englewood Cliffs, N.J.: Prentice-Hall, 1966.

———. *Primitive Social Organization: An Evolutionary Perspective.* New York: Random House, 1962.

Shapiro, Harry L., ed. *Man, Culture, and Society.* New York: Oxford University Press, 1956.

Smith, Frank, and Miller, George A., eds. *The Genesis of Language: A Psycholinguistic Approach.* Cambridge: M.I.T. Press, 1966.

Southwick, Charles H., ed. *Primate Social Behavior: An Enduring Problem, Selected Readings.* Princeton, N.J.: Van Nostrand, 1963.

Spuhler, J. N., ed. *The Evolution of Man's Capacity for Culture.* Detroit, Mich.: Wayne State University Press, 1959.

Steward, Julian H. *Theory of Culture Change.* Urbana: University of Illinois Press, 1955.

————. "Evolutionary Principles and Social Types," in Sol Tax, ed., *Evolution After Darwin,* Vol. 2, *The Evolution of Man: Man, Culture, and Society.* Chicago: University of Chicago Press, 1960, pp. 169–86.

Tax, Sol, ed. *Evolution After Darwin,* Vol. 2, *The Evolution of Man: Man, Culture, and Society.* Chicago: University of Chicago Press, 1960.

————, ed. *Horizons of Anthropology.* Chicago: Aldine, 1964.

Van Lawiek-Goodall, Jane. *My Friends the Wild Chimpanzees.* Washington, D.C.: National Geographic Society, 1967.

Wagner, Philip. *The Human Use of the Earth: An Examination of the Interaction Between Man and His Physical Environment.* New York: Free Press, 1960.

Washburn, Sherwood L. "An Ape's Eye-View of Human Evolution," in Paul L. DeVore, ed., *The Origin of Man.* New York: Wenner-Gren Foundation for Anthropological Research, 1965, pp. 38–96.

————, ed. *Classification and Human Evolution.* Chicago: Aldine, 1963.

————, ed. *Social Life of Early Man.* Chicago: Aldine, 1961.

————. "Tools and Human Evolution." *Scientific American,* Vol. 203 (1960), pp. 62–75.

————, and Avis, Virginia. "Evolution of Human Behavior," in Anne Roe and George Gaylord Simpson, eds., *Behavior and Evolution.* New Haven: Yale University Press, 1958, pp. 421–36.

————, and Howell, F. Clark. "Human Evolution and Culture," in Sol Tax, ed., *Evolution After Darwin*, Vol. 2, *The Evolution of Man: Man, Culture, and Society*. Chicago: University of Chicago Press, 1960, pp. 33–56.

Watson, Patty Jo. "Clues to Iranian Prehistory in Modern Village Life." *Expedition*, Vol. 3 (1966), pp. 9–19.

Watson, Richard A. "Is Geology Different?" *Philosophy of Science*, Vol. 33 (1966), pp. 172–85.

White, Leslie A. *The Evolution of Culture: The Development of Civilization to the Fall of Rome*. New York: McGraw-Hill, 1959.

————. *The Science of Culture: A Study of Man and Civilization*. New York: Farrar, Straus, 1949.

Wolf, Eric R. *Peasants*. Englewood Cliffs, N.J.: Prentice-Hall, 1966.

Wright, Gary A. *Obsidian Analysis and Prehistoric Near Eastern Trade: 7500 to 3500 B.C.* Ann Arbor: University of Michigan Press, 1969.

Wright, Herbert E., Jr. "The Natural Environment of Early Food Production in the Mountains North of Mesopotamia." *Science*, Vol. 161 (1968), pp. 161 and 334–39.

Zeuner, Frederick E. *A History of Domesticated Animals*. New York: Harper & Row, 1963.